The Complete Private Pilot

Syllabus

Flight and Ground Training
Private Pilot Certification Course: Airplane
Meets 14 CFR Part 141 and Part 61 Requirements

Second Edition

Aviation Supplies and Academics, Inc.
7005 132nd Place SE
Newcastle, WA 98059-3153

The Complete Private Pilot Syllabus
© 1994–2003 Aviation Supplies & Academics, Inc.

This syllabus is designed to be used with the textbook,
The Complete Private Pilot, by Bob Gardner.

Aviation Supplies & Academics, Inc.
7005 132nd Place SE
Newcastle, Washington 98059-3153
Email: asa@asa2fly.com
Web: www.asa2fly.com

Printed in the United States of America

06 05   9 8 7 6 5 4 3 2

ISBN 1-56027-526-X
ASA-PPT-S2

Contents

	Page
Student Information	v
Introduction	vii
Private Pilot Course Hours	viii

Stage 1: Solo Flight 1

Flight Lesson 1	2
Ground Lesson 1	3
Flight Lesson 2	4
Flight Lesson 3	6
Ground Lesson 2	8
Flight Lesson 4	9
Flight Lesson 5	11
Ground Lesson 3	12
Flight Lesson 6	13
Flight Lesson 7 (Pre-Solo Exam)	14
Ground Lesson 4 (Stage 1 Exam)	15
Flight Lesson 8	16
Solo Endorsements	17
Flight Lesson 9 (Stage 1 Check)	18

Stage 2: Cross-Country 19

Ground Lesson 5	20
Flight Lesson 10	21
Flight Lesson 11	23
Ground Lesson 6	24
Flight Lesson 12	25
Alternate Airport Endorsement	26
Flight Lesson 13	26
Ground Lesson 7	27
Flight Lesson 14	28
Flight Lesson 15	29
Ground Lesson 8	30

Flight Lesson 16 31

Flight Lesson 17 32

Ground Lesson 9 (Stage 2 Exam) 34

Flight Lesson 18 35

Cross-Country Endorsements 36

Flight Lesson 19 (Stage 2 Check) 37

Stage 3: Pilot Operations 39

Ground Lesson 10 40

Flight Lesson 20 41

Flight Lesson 21 42

Ground Lesson 11 43

Flight Lesson 22 43

Flight Lesson 23 44

Ground Lesson 12 (Stage 3 Exam and Final Exam) 45

Flight Lesson 24 (Stage 3 Check) 45

Flight Lesson 25 46

Private Pilot Endorsements 47

Checkride Checklist 47

Pre-Solo Exam 49

Stage Exams 53

Stage 1 Exam 53

Stage 2 Exam 65

Stage 3 Exam 79

Final Exam 85

Maps 99

Appendix Appendix–1

Answers to Exam Questions Appendix–3

Enrollment Certificate Appendix–5

Graduation Certificate Appendix–5

Private Pilot Certificate Application (FAA Form 8710-1) Appendix–6

Student Information

Name _____
       Last   *First*   *Middle*

Address _____
      Street (If mailing address is P.O. Box, please list both.)

_____
City   *State*   *Zip*   *Country*

Private Pilot course enrollment date _____
                                    Date

Enrollment notice to FAA (Part 141)_____
                                    Date

Student Pilot/Medical Certificate:

   Issue Date _____ Class _____

Previous School _____

Training credit transfer _____ _____
                         Flight   *Ground*

Phone _____ _____ _____
       Home   *Business*   *Other*

Emergency contact _____

   Phone Number(s) _____

Record of Aircraft Checkouts

Date	Make/Model	Instructor Signature
_____	_____	_____
_____	_____	_____
_____	_____	_____

Remarks _____

_____

Record of Course Completion

FAA Private Pilot Knowledge Examination _____ _____
                                       Date   *Score*

Graduation Certificate _____
                    Date Issued

Private Pilot Practical Test _____ _____
                        Date   *Results*

Introduction

The Complete Private Pilot Syllabus is designed to work with *The Complete Private Pilot* (Ninth Edition) by Bob Gardner. This textbook can be used in the ground training sessions outlined in Stages 1-3. In addition, recommended readings from ASA's *Private Pilot Test Prep* are given for the ground training sessions.

Enrollment Prerequisites

The student must be able to read, speak, write, and understand the English language and meet the physical standards for a third-class medical certificate prior to enrollment, and must possess a valid student pilot certificate and a third-class medical certificate (or higher) prior to completion of Flight Lesson 8, Stage 1. Students must be 16 years old to solo, and 17 years old to earn a private pilot certificate.

Training Course Objectives

The student will obtain the aeronautical skill and experience necessary to meet the requirements of a **private pilot** certificate with an **airplane** category and **single-engine land** class rating, and the aeronautical knowledge necessary to pass the FAA Knowledge Exam.

Course Completion Standards

The student will demonstrate through flight tests, written tests, and school records the necessary aeronautical skill, knowledge, and experience to pass the FAA Private Pilot Knowledge Exam and obtain a **private pilot** certificate with an **airplane** category and a **single-engine land** class rating. Each Task under each Area of Operation in the *Private Pilot Practical Test Standards* will have been accomplished by the student.

The instructor will not sign off any Task until the student is able to explain and/or demonstrate the elements of the procedure or maneuver as required by the Practical Test Standards.

Training Syllabus

The 35.0 hours of flight training and 35.0 hours of ground training, as required by 14 CFR Part 141 (40.0 hours of flight training and no minimum time for ground training is specified for Part 61 programs) will be accomplished in three stages. Each of these instructional units is described in the following pages. The aeronautical experience must include 35.0 hours in an airplane; however, a ground training device acceptable to the Administrator of the Federal Aviation Administration may be substituted for 20 percent of the required time if the ground trainer complies with 14 CFR Part 141.41(a), and may be substituted for 15 percent of the required time if the ground trainer complies with 14 CFR Part 141.41(b).

Hours shown for each lesson for flight training, preflight briefing, and post-flight critique are offered as a guide to the instructor. Specified minimum times for an entire stage must be complied with, but time used for an individual lesson may be adjusted to the student's needs. The instructor is responsible for ensuring all requirements are met.

At points where normal student progress should meet the requirements of the Practical Test Standards for a Task included in an Area of Operation, the Area of Operation and Task are listed under Completion Standards; however, it is not mandatory that the instructor sign off the Task in order for the lesson to be considered complete.

Private Pilot Course Hours

This syllabus complies with 14 CFR Part 141 requirements. To follow a Part 61 curriculum, add 5 hours of solo flight time, for a total of 40 hours. Part 61 requires 10 hours of solo time, including 5 hours of solo cross-country (with the long cross-country being 150 NM).

Ground instruction for Flight Lessons include preflight briefings and post-flight critiques.

*14 CFR Part 141 requires 20 hours of dual flight, 5 hours of solo flight, and a total of 35 hours flight time for the Private Pilot Certificate. Those flights tagged with an asterisk (*) indicate the flights which may be conducted either Dual or Solo, at the instructor's discretion.

Flight	Dual Flight	Solo Flight	Dual X/C	Solo X/C	Dual Night	Solo Night	Instrument Instruction	Ground Instruction
Stage 1								
Flight 1	1.0							1.0
Ground 1								1.5
Flight 2	1.0							0.5
Flight 3	1.0						0.25	0.5
Ground 2								1.5
Flight 4	1.0						0.25	0.5
Flight 5	1.0						0.25	0.5
Ground 3								1.5
Flight 6	1.0							0.5
Flight 7	1.0						0.25	0.5 + Pre-Solo Exam
Ground 4								1.5 + Stage 1 Exam
Flight 8	0.5	0.5						0.5
Flight 9 Stage Check	1.0						0.25	0.5
Stage 2								
Ground 5								1.5
Flight 10	1.5						0.25	0.5
Flight 11	0.5	0.5						0.5
Ground 6								1.5
Flight 12		1.0*						0.5
Flight 13		1.5						0.5
Ground 7								1.5
Flight 14		1.0*						0.5
Flight 15	1.0						0.25	0.5

Flight	Dual Flight	Solo Flight	Dual X/C	Solo X/C	Dual Night	Solo Night	Instrument Instruction	Ground Instruction
Stage 2	(cont.)							
Ground 8								1.5
Flight 16	1.0		1.0				0.25	1.0
Flight 17	2.0		2.0		2.0 (includes 5 TOL)			1.0
Ground 9								1.5+ Stage 2 Exam
Flight 18		2.5		2.5 (>100 NM, 3 TOL at towered airport)				1.0
Flight 19 Stage Check	1.0				1.0 (includes 5 TOL)		0.25	0.5
Stage 3								
Ground 10								1.5
Flight 20		3.0*		3.0*				1.0
Flight 21		4.0*		4.0*				1.0
Ground 11								1.5
Flight 22	1.5						0.25	0.5
Flight 23		1.0*						1.0
Ground 12								1.5 + Stage 3 Exam + Final Exam
Flight 24 Stage Check	1.5						0.25	1.0
Flight 25	1.5						0.25	1.0
Totals 40 hrs (Part 61) 35 hrs (Part 141)	**20.0†** +10* optional	**5.0•** +10* optional	**3.0**	**2.5◊**	**3.0≠**		**3.0**	**35.0**

† Includes 3 hours prep for checkride.
• Part 61 programs require 10 hours of solo flight.
◊ Including 1 X/C more than 100 NM, 3 points for Part 141 programs. Part 61 programs require 5.0 hours solo X/C, with the long flight being 150 NM.
≠ Including 1 X/C of more than 100 NM and 10 takeoffs and landings (TOL).

Stage 1: Solo Flight

Flight Training

8.5 Hours Dual (1.25 Hours Instrument)
0.5 Hour Solo

Objectives

The student will be instructed in all the basic flying procedures and skills necessary for the first solo flight.

Completion Standards

The Stage will be completed when the student satisfactorily passes the Stage 1 check and is able to conduct solo flights.

Ground Training

11.0 Hours
Pre-Solo Exam
Stage 1 Exam

Objective

In Stage 1 the student will be introduced to a typical general aviation airplane, learn the airplane's parts and how it is constructed. The student will learn the basics of aerodynamics, will be introduced to airplane engines and instruments, will learn how to perform weight and balance calculations, and how to use handbook information to predict aircraft performance.

Completion Standards

Stage 1 will be complete when the student has taken the Stage 1 written examination and has achieved a minimum passing score of 80 percent. The instructor will discuss and resolve all incorrect answers with the student before going on to Stage 2.

Flight Lesson 1

Dual 1.0 Hour
Pre/Postflight 1.0 Hour

Objectives

The student will be familiarized with the aircraft, its operating characteristics, cabin controls, instruments, systems, preflight procedures, use of checklists, and safety precautions. The student will practice climbs, straight-and-level flight, turns, and descents.

Content

1. Preflight discussion

2. Preflight inspection
    a. Aircraft status—maintenance writeups, etc.
    b. Aircraft and engine logbooks, inspection status
    c. External inspection
    d. Servicing procedures—fuel grade, oil type and quantity
    e. Ground handling and safety; propeller cautions
    f. Required documents—AROW
    g. Placards and limitation markings
    h. Seat adjustment and check of locking mechanism
    i. Hobbs meter/tachometer entries
    j. Stowage of tow bar, etc.
    k. All doors and hatches secured

3. Introduction
    a. Special Emphasis Areas discussion: positive aircraft control, positive exchange of flight controls, stall/spin awareness, collision avoidance, wake turbulence avoidance, LAHSO, runway incursion avoidance, controlled flight into terrain, aeronautical decision making, checklist usage.
    b. Starting and taxiing
    c. Runup; significance of items checked
    d. Takeoff, pattern departure, and initial climb
    e. Level off; straight-and-level flight; trim
    f. Medium banked turns
    g. Descents
    h. Traffic pattern entry, approach and landing
    i. Radio communication; microphone use
    j. Climbing turns (VR and IR)
        (1) Left-turning tendency; torque factors
        (2) Relate 10° bank (IR) to natural horizon
        (3) Rudder use for entry and recovery from banked flight

4. Fill out enrollment certificate. *See Page Appendix–5.*

5. Postflight critique and preview of next lesson

Completion Standards

The student will be able to maintain straight-and-level flight with a tolerance of ±200 feet in altitude and ±20° in heading, to perform climbs, descents, turn entries and turn recoveries with proper rudder use (1/2 ball width), and to explain proper control use for straight-and-level flight, turns, climbs, and descents. The student will understand and be able to explain pitch, bank, and airspeed limits.

Date of completion _____ Time flown _____

Instructor signature _____ Student initials _____

Ground Lesson 1

1.5 Hours

Reading Assignment
The Complete Private Pilot, Lesson 1

Lesson Content
Fuselage construction
Airplane components
Lift development; components of the lift equation
Lift, thrust, and drag
Axes of rotation; center of lift vs. center of gravity
Control effects
Stability, longitudinal and lateral
Turn dynamics
Stalls and spins

Date of completion _____ Lesson time _____

Instructor signature _____ Student initials _____

Recommended Reading: *Private Pilot Test Prep,* Chapter 1

Flight Lesson 2

Dual 1.0 Hour
Pre/Postflight 0.5 Hour

Objectives

The student will review the maneuvers covered in Lesson 1. The instructor will introduce climbing turns, slow flight, power-off stalls, and steep turns, as exercises in coordination.

Content

1. Preflight discussion
2. Starting and taxiing
   a. Use of checklist
   b. Engine start (discuss priming and flooded starts)
   c. Runup and pre-takeoff checklist. Student explains each action
3. Takeoff and departure; initial climb
   a. Application of power; rudder use
   b. Takeoff trim; elevator use and takeoff attitude
   c. Clearing turns while climbing
4. Straight-and-level flight
   a. Attitude, power setting and airspeed
   b. Use of trim
   c. Speed changes in level flight
5. Climbing turns (VR and IR)
   a. Use of attitude indicator banking scale vs. natural horizon
   b. Pitch and power coordination during entry
   c. Rudder use in left vs. right turns
   d. Pitch and power coordination during recovery
6. Slow flight
   a. Pitch and power relationship
   b. Use of flaps and flap limit speeds
   c. Loss of visibility at high pitch attitudes
   d. Recovery to cruise flight
   e. Power curve—lift vs. drag
7. Power-off stalls
   a. Clearing turns
   b. Recovery without power
   c. Recovery with power
   d. Effect of flaps on indicated stall speed
8. Steep turns
   a. Use of elevator and power
   b. Overbanking tendency
9. Approach and landing
10. Postflight critique and preview of next lesson

Completion Standards

The student will be able to use checklists, start the engine, taxi, and perform the preflight runup without assistance; take off and climb at the recommended climb speed ±10 knots; maintain level flight within ±150 feet of altitude and ±15° of heading; perform coordinated climbing turn entries and recoveries to the same tolerances; and recognize and recover from power-off stalls with or without power.

Practical Test Standards

I. Preflight Preparation

   A. Certificates and Documents

   B. Airworthiness Requirements

II. Preflight Procedures

   A. Preflight Inspection

   B. Cockpit Management

XII. Postflight Procedures

   A. After Landing, Parking and Securing

Date of completion _____ Time flown _____

Instructor signature _____ Student initials _____

Flight Lesson 3

Dual 1.0 Hour (0.25 Hour Instrument)
Pre/Postflight 0.5 Hour

Objectives

The student will demonstrate proficiency in the four basic maneuvers and perform, without assistance, slow flight, power-off stalls, and steep turns. The student will further explore the full regime of flight through the introduction of slips, use of flaps, and climbs and descents with various combinations of pitch, power, airspeed, and flap extension. The student will assume pilot-in-command responsibility for preflight, taxi, and runup operation.

Content

1. Preflight discussion
2. Review and practice
   a. Takeoff, departure, climb, and climbing turns (VR and IR)
   b. Level off and straight-and-level flight (VR and IR)
   c. Medium banked turns (VR and IR)
   d. Traffic pattern, approach and landing
3. Introduction
   a. Slips
      (1) Bank angle vs. rudder pressure in cruise and slow flight
      (2) Sideslips and forward slips
      (3) Slipping as a steep approach technique
   b. Flap use (VR and IR)
      (1) Flap extension in slow flight at constant altitude and airspeed
      (2) Flap extension in slow flight at constant altitude and power
      (3) Flap extension in transitioning from cruise to slow flight
      (4) Loss of lift due to flap retraction
      (5) Simulated go-around from landing configuration
   c. Climbs and descents (VR and IR)
      (1) Constant airspeed climb by increasing power
      (2) Constant power climb with reduced airspeed
      (3) Constant airspeed descent by reducing power
      (4) Constant power descent with increasing airspeed
      (5) Constant rate, constant airspeed climb
      (6) Constant rate, constant airspeed descent
      (7) Power-off descent at best glide speed
   d. Slow flight (VR and IR)
      (1) Slowing to approach speed
      (2) Pitch and power relationship
      (3) Maneuvering during slow flight and the region of reversed command
      (4) Turn rate vs. bank angle at low airspeeds
      (5) Control effectiveness and feel
      (6) Adverse aileron drag and yaw

e. Power-off stalls (VR and IR)
   (1) Straight ahead—recognition and recovery
   (2) Turning—recognition and recovery
   (3) Emphasis on changing elevator deflection and pressure needed to maintain pitch attitude prior to stall and relation to landing attitude
f. Approach and traffic pattern
   (1) Visual scanning pattern for collision avoidance
   (2) Speed adjustment for spacing from other traffic
   (3) Relation of pattern to runway and wind
   (4) Key position and consistency of airspeed and altitude
   (5) Power adjustment and flap use
   (6) Visual clues for beginning the flare
   (7) Touchdown attitude
4. Postflight critique and preview of next lesson

Completion Standards

The student will perform all maneuvers from previous lessons with tolerances of ±150 feet in altitude, ±15° in heading, ±5 knots in airspeed with l/2-ball-width maximum deflection. Climbs, descents, and slips will be accomplished within ±10 knots, ±200 FPM, ±20° in the various configuration, with student anticipation of pitch changes and/or pressures necessary to prevent unnecessary pitch variations. The student will promptly trim off all unnecessary control pressures, and demonstrate prompt decision-making when required.

Practical Test Standards

II: Preflight Procedures

   C. Engine Starting
   D. Taxiing
   F. Before Takeoff Check

IV: Takeoffs, Landings, and Go-Arounds

   A. Normal Takeoff and Climb

Date of completion _____ Time flown _____

Instructor signature _____ Student initials _____

Ground Lesson 2

1.5 Hours

Reading Assignment
The Complete Private Pilot, Lessons 2 and 3

Lesson Content
The 4-cycle engine
Ignition
Induction systems
Fuel systems
Mixture control
Fuel grade and contamination
Preignition and detonation
Engine instrumentation
Electrical and vacuum systems
Constant speed propellers
Turbocharging
Pressurization
Rotax engines
Pitot-static instruments
Gyroscopic instruments
Magnetic compass

Date of completion _____ Lesson time _____

Instructor signature _____ Student initials _____

Recommended Reading: *Private Pilot Test Prep,* Chapter 2

Flight Lesson 4

Dual 1.0 Hour (0.25 Hour Instrument)
Pre/Postflight 0.5 Hour

Objectives

During this lesson the student will further explore the limits of airplane performance, with the added complexity of left-turning tendency, G-loading and various flap configurations. The student will transition naturally into these maneuvers from the review of previously learned maneuvers: slow flight is pursued beyond its limit into power-on stalls; steep turns and slow flight are combined to produce accelerated stalls; glides, speed changes, and flap extension are combined, as on an approach, until an approach-to-landing stall develops. This lesson will emphasize not only recognition and recovery from stalls but also the situations which lead to inadvertent stalls. Power-off glides will be reviewed, with engine failure emergency procedures introduced. Wind effects will be investigated through the introduction of crosswind/downwind taxi techniques and elementary ground reference maneuvers.

Content

1. Preflight discussion
2. Review and practice
    a. Takeoff, departure, climbing turns (VR and IR)
    b. Level off and straight-and-level flight (VR and IR)
    c. Medium turns (VR and IR)
    d. Maneuvering during slow flight (VR and IR)
    e. Slips and descents
    f. Traffic pattern, approach, and landing
3. Introduction
    a. Taxiing with crosswind/tailwind
       (1) Control use
       (2) Speed control and brake use
       (3) Weathervaning in turns
    b. Power-on stalls
       (1) Turning tendency
       (2) Rudder use
       (3) Control effectiveness
       (4) Adverse yaw
       (5) Rolling tendency
       (6) Attitude and directional control
       (7) Attitude and elevator force for recovery; overpowering trim if required
    c. Accelerated stalls (VR and IR)
       (1) G-loading vs. stall speed
       (2) Turning stalls
       (3) Secondary stalls
    d. Approach-to-landing stalls
       (1) Simulate traffic pattern
       (2) Straight ahead
       (3) Turning
       (4) Effect of flaps

Continued

    e. Elementary forced landings
        (1) Best glide speed
        (2) Trim
        (3) Selection of landing site
        (4) Troubleshooting; restarting engine
        (5) Communications
        (6) Shut down procedures
    f. Ground reference maneuvers
        (1) Tracking a straight line
        (2) Rectangular course
        (3) Tracking a runway—forward slip method
    g. Collision avoidance
        (1) Outside cockpit vision
        (2) Scanning patterns
        (3) Aircraft lighting
        (4) Right-of-way rules
4. Postflight critique and preview of next lesson

Completion Standards

Successful completion requires the student to perform all maneuvers from previous lessons without assistance. The student will recognize and promptly recover from the newly introduced stalls, without assistance or loss of control. The student should begin anticipating and making corrections for the effect of wind on the aircraft's ground track and understand basic emergency procedures. Altitude, airspeed, and heading tolerances remain in force.

Practical Test Standards

I: Preflight Preparation

G. Operation of Systems

III: Airport Operations

A. Radio Communications and ATC Light Signals
B. Traffic Patterns

V: Performance Maneuver

A. Steep Turns

IX: Basic Instrument Maneuvers

A. Straight-and-Level Flight
B. Constant Airspeed Climbs
C. Constant Airspeed Descents
D. Turns to Headings

Date of completion _____ Time flown _____

Instructor signature _____ Student initials _____

Flight Lesson 5

Dual 1.0 Hour (0.25 Hour Instrument)
Pre/Postflight 0.5 Hour

Objectives

This lesson will consist of a review of previously learned maneuvers, a deeper investigation into the control of wind effect through variations in bank angle and turn rate during ground-reference maneuvers, and the introduction of takeoff/departure stalls and go-around procedures. The student should be in full command of the aircraft and display confidence in his/her ability to control it through the entire flight regime.

Content

1. Preflight discussion
2. Review and practice
   a. Slow flight (VR and IR)
   b. Medium turns (VR and IR)
   c. Stalls, straight and turning
      (1) Power-off
      (2) Power-on
      (3) Accelerated
   d. Simulated forced landing
   e. Basic ground reference maneuvers
   f. Traffic pattern, approach and landing
3. Introduction
   a. Takeoff/departure stalls
      (1) Trim induced stalls
      (2) Reducing angle of attack without unnecessary altitude loss
      (3) Secondary stall
   b. Aborted landings
      (1) Power use and turning tendency at low airspeed
      (2) Flap retraction
      (3) Clearing runway and climbing traffic
      (4) Obstacle clearance
   c. Ground reference maneuvers
      (1) S-turns
      (2) Turns around a point
   d. Steep turns (VR and IR)
      (1) Relationship of back pressure to bank angle; induced drag
      (2) Effect of pitch changes on VSI and altimeter
      (3) Overbanking tendency
      (4) Correction and recovery techniques
      (5) Emphasis on sensory perception of G-loads
4. Postflight critique and preview of next lesson

Continued

Completion Standards

The student should perform all maneuvers without hesitation, maintain control of the aircraft at all times, and be capable of evaluating his/her own performance. The student should be able to correct ground track for wind effect, and cope with a simulated engine failure. Tolerances are airspeed ±10 knots, altitude ±100 feet, heading ±10°.

Practical Test Standards

IV: Takeoffs, Landings, and Go-Arounds

    K. Forward Slips to a Landing

    L. Go-Around

VIII: Slow Flight and Stalls

    A. Maneuvering During Slow Flight

Date of completion _____ Time flown _____

Instructor signature _____ Student initials _____

Ground Lesson 3

1.5 Hours

Reading Assignment

The Complete Private Pilot, Lesson 8

Lesson Content

Importance of CG position
Effects of overloading
Weight x Arm = Moment
Weight and balance calculations, tabular method
Weight and balance calculations, graphic method

Date of completion _____ Lesson time _____

Instructor signature _____ Student initials _____

Recommended Reading: *Private Pilot Test Prep,* Chapter 3

Flight Lesson 6

Dual 1.0 Hour
Pre/Postflight 0.5 Hour

Objectives

This lesson will review slow flight, weak areas from previous lessons, and traffic pattern entry procedures, in preparation for the introduction of concentrated work on takeoffs and landings. The second phase of the lesson will consist of takeoffs and landings with special emphasis on establishment of consistent traffic pattern procedures, airspeed and ground track control, use of power and flaps in descent, glide path control, and visual clues for landing.

Content

1. Preflight discussion
2. Review and practice
   a. Slow flight
   b. Traffic pattern entry
   c. Selected maneuvers
3. Introduction
   a. Takeoff and landing
      (1) Rotation speed; best angle and best rate climbs
      (2) Rudder use during takeoff run and initial climb
      (3) Ground effect during takeoff
      (4) Level off
      (5) Maintaining ground track
      (6) Key points in the pattern
      (7) Effect of wind on pattern size
      (8) Power reduction and initial descent
      (9) Use of trim
      (10) Flap use; limiting speeds
      (11) Approach airspeed
      (12) Glide path control
      (13) Visual clues for landing
      (14) Ground effect during the flare
      (15) Landing attitude
4. Postflight critique and preview of next lesson

Completion Standards

The student should be able to perform all previously learned maneuvers to flight test standards and be able to apply these maneuvers and techniques to the task of flying the aircraft through a reasonably precise traffic pattern, approach, and landing.

Continued

Practical Test Standards
VI: Ground Reference Maneuvers

  A. Rectangular Course

Date of completion _____ Time flown _____

Instructor signature _____ Student initials _____

Flight Lesson 7

Dual 1.0 Hour (0.25 Hour Instrument)
Pre/Postflight 0.5 Hour + Pre-Solo Exam

Objectives

This lesson will afford the student continued practice on takeoffs and landings. The instructor will gradually introduce techniques to improve performance under various field and wind conditions such as crosswinds, slips, no-flap approaches, rejected takeoffs, and emergency go-arounds.

Content

1. Preflight discussion
2. Review and practice
3. Introduction
   a. Rejected takeoff
      (1) Go/no-go decision point
      (2) Deceleration procedures
   b. Emergency go-around
      (1) Land/go-around decision point
      (2) Power and flap use
      (3) Left-turning tendency during climb
      (4) Re-entering the traffic pattern
   c. Emergencies in the traffic pattern
      (1) Engine failure after takeoff (discussion)
      (2) Engine failure in the pattern
      (3) Change in wind direction/runway in use (discussion)
      (4) Closure of airport or runway while airborne (discussion)
4. Postflight critique and preview of next lesson

Completion Standards

The student should fly a precise traffic pattern, compensate for wind effect on ground track and glide path, maintain spacing from other aircraft, make safe judgments and control the aircraft in unusual or unanticipated situations, and make unassisted takeoffs and landings.

Practical Test Standards

IV: Takeoffs, Landings, and Go-Arounds

B. Normal Approach and Landing

Date of completion _____ Time flown _____

Instructor signature _____ Student initials _____

Ground Lesson 4

1.5 Hour
Stage 1 Exam

Reading Assignment

The Complete Private Pilot, Lesson 8

Lesson Content

Density altitude
Takeoff and climb performance
Best angle, best rate-of-climb
Cruise performance
Landing distance
Ground effect

Date of completion _____ Lesson time _____

Instructor signature _____ Student initials _____

8Recommended Reading: *Private Pilot Test Prep,* Chapter 8

Flight Lesson 8:

Dual 0.5 Hour
Solo 0.5 Hour
Pre/Postflight 0.5 Hour

Objectives

At the completion of the dual portion of the lesson, the student will have demonstrated proficiency in all phases of traffic pattern operations, takeoffs, and landings under varying conditions. During this portion the instructor will review and test the student's ability to think through unusual or emergency situations and ensure that the student is prepared for changes in aircraft performance due to weight change when solo. Three solo takeoffs and landings to a full stop are to be performed.

Content

1. Preflight discussion
   a. Pre-solo oral examination
   b. Check for current medical and endorse student certificate and logbook
2. Review and practice
   a. Takeoff
   b. Traffic pattern
   c. Radio communications
   d. Approach and landing
   e. Emergencies and go-arounds
3. Introduction
   a. Briefing on radio use
   b. Supervised solo in traffic pattern
   c. Three solo takeoffs and landings
4. Postflight critique and preview of next lesson

Completion Standards

The student should demonstrate judgment and capability as pilot-in-command, as well as the skill required to take off and land the airplane, prior to be being permitted to solo. Three satisfactory solo takeoffs and full-stop landings will be observed.

Practical Test Standards

III: Airport Operations

   C. Airport, Runway and Taxiway Signs, Markings and Lighting

X: Emergency Operations

   A. Emergency Approach and Landing
   C. Emergency Equipment and Survival Gear

Date of completion _____ Time flown _____

Instructor signature _____ Student initials _____

Solo Endorsements

Instructor Note: Follow the formats below when signing-off endorsements for your students (from AC 61-65D). Instructor will also need to endorse student pilot certificate.

1. **Endorsement for pre-solo aeronautical knowledge: 14 CFR § 61.87(b)**

   I certify that (*First name, MI, Last name*) has satisfactorily completed the presolo knowledge exam of §61.87(b) for the (*make and model aircraft*).

   S/S   [date]   J.J. Jones   987654321 CFI   Exp. 12-31-00

2. **Endorsement for pre-solo flight training: 14 CFR § 61.87(c)**

   I certify that (*First name, MI, Last name*) has received the required presolo training in a (make and model aircraft). I have determined he/she has demonstrated the proficiency of §61.87(d) and is proficient to make solo flights in (*make and model aircraft*).

   S/S   [date]   J.J. Jones   987654321 CFI   Exp. 12-31-00

3. **Endorsement for solo (each additional 90-day period): 14 CFR § 61.87(m)**

   I certify that (*First name, MI, Last name*) has received the required training to qualify for solo flying. I have determined he/she meets the applicable requirements of §61.87(n) and is proficient to make solo flights in (*make and model*).

   S/S   [date]   J.J. Jones   987654321 CFI   Exp. 12-31-00

4. **Endorsement for solo flight in the Class B airspace: 14 CFR § 61.95(a)**

   I certify that (*First name, MI, Last name*) has received the required training of §61.95(a). I have determined he/she is proficient to conduct solo flights in (*name of Class B*) airspace. (*List any applicable conditions or limitations.*)

   S/S   [date]   J.J. Jones   987654321 CFI   Exp. 12-31-00

5. **Endorsement for solo flight to, from, or at an airport located within Class B airspace: 14 CFR § 61.95(b) and 91.131(b)(1)(ii)**

   I certify that (*First name, MI, Last name*) has received the required training of §61.95(a)(1). I have determined that he/she is proficient to conduct solo flight operations at (*name of airport*). (*List any applicable conditions or limitations.*)

   S/S   [date]   J.J. Jones   987654321 CFI   Exp. 12-31-00

Flight Lesson 9: Stage Check

Dual 1.0 Hour (0.25 Hour Instrument)
Pre/Postflight 0.5 Hour

Objectives

During this flight the Chief Flight Instructor or the assistant Chief Flight Instructor will confirm the student's ability to conduct solo flights and exercise the judgment required for unsupervised operations.

Content

1. Evaluation—any maneuvers from Stage 1 lessons may be included
2. Postflight critique

Completion Standards

1. Maintain altitude ±100 feet
2. Maintain heading ±10 degrees
3. Maintain airspeed ±10 knots
4. Maintain coordinated control of the aircraft
5. Display reasonable skill and understanding in the execution of Stage 1 maneuvers and procedures.

Date of completion _____ Time flown _____

Instructor signature _____ Student initials _____

Stage 2: Cross-Country

Flight Training

7.0 Hours Dual
(3 Hours Cross-Country, 3 Hours Night, 1.0 Hour Instrument)
6.5 Hours Solo (2 hours may be conducted Dual at the instructor's discretion)
(2.5 Hours Cross-Country)

Objectives

The student will learn how to plan and conduct cross-country flights using pilotage, dead reckoning, and radio navigation, will learn how to use ATC services under VFR conditions, and will learn the techniques and procedures of night flying.

Completion Standards

The stage will be completed when the student has demonstrated that he/she can plan and conduct solo cross-country flights using pilotage, dead reckoning, and radio navigation under VFR conditions, and can obtain and evaluate weather forecasts, reports, and actual flight conditions to determine that VFR flight can be safely conducted.

Ground Training

14.0 Hours
Stage 2 Exam

Objective

In Stage 2 the student will learn how to navigate by pilotage and dead reckoning, how radio navigation is used in the National Airspace System, how to communicate effectively and efficiently. The student will learn about operations at both small fields and large airports, and will receive a thorough primer in weather fundamentals as well as how pilots obtain weather information.

Completion Standards

Stage 2 will be complete when the student has taken and passed the Stage 2 written examination with a passing grade of 80% and has discussed and resolved any incorrect answers with the instructor.

Ground Lesson 5

1.5 Hours

Reading Assignment
The Complete Private Pilot, Lesson 9

Lesson Content
Aeronautical charts
Geographical coordinates
Time zones
Statute vs. nautical miles
Magnetic variation and deviation
Wind drift correction
Use of flight computers
Groundspeed vs. airspeed
Chart reading
Flight planning

Date of completion _____ Lesson time _____

Instructor signature _____ Student initials _____

Recommended Reading: *Private Pilot Test Prep,* Chapter 9

Flight Lesson 10

Dual 1.5 Hours (0.25 Hour Instrument)
Pre/Postflight 0.5 Hour

Objectives

The student will learn how to use the flight and navigation instruments in preparation for cross-country flying, and will be instructed in recovery from unusual attitudes by instrument reference only, in DF steers, and in ASR approach techniques.

Content

1. Preflight discussion

    a. Instrument design, indications, and limitations
    b. Pitot and vacuum systems

2. Introduction

    a. Use of the turn coordinator
        (1) Standard rate turns
        (2) Timed turns
    b. Use of the magnetic compass
        (1) Influence of nearby ferrous metal and electric wiring
        (2) Oscillation error; averaging in turbulence
        (3) Acceleration and deceleration errors
        (4) Northerly turning error
    c. Precision turns to headings
        (1) Updating heading indicator to magnetic compass reading
        (2) Leading rollout (1/2 bank angle)
        (3) Bank angle vs. heading change
        (4) Pitch control during turns
    d. Use of VOR
        (1) Navigation radio controls
        (2) Tuning and identifying VOR stations
        (3) VOR and the sectional chart
        (4) VOR orientation
        (5) Intercepting and tracking radials and bearings
        (6) Fixing position using dual VORs
        (7) Failure indications
        (8) Station passage
    e. Use of ADF
        (1) Radio controls
        (2) Tuning and identifying
        (3) Orientation
    f. Recovery from unusual attitudes
        (1) Inducing vertigo; discussion and demonstration
        (2) Recovery from steep climbing turn
        (3) Recovery from power-on spiral
        (4) Recovery from inverted flight (simulator only)

Continued

g. Inadvertent loss of visual reference
   (1) Level 180° turn
   (2) Climb to VFR conditions or safe altitude
   (3) Controlled emergency descent
   (4) Communications for radar or DF steers
h. ASR approach (simulator or actual if available)
   (1) Precise heading control
   (2) Standard and 1/2-standard rate turns
   (3) Transition to approach speed
   (4) Controlling descent rate
   (5) Controller terminology
3. Postflight critique and preview of next lesson

Completion Standards

The student will demonstrate the ability to use the magnetic compass, turn and slip indicator, and heading indicator to fly selected headings. A tolerance of ±5 degrees will be allowed when all instruments are used. The student will demonstrate understanding of the VOR and the ability to intercept and fly selected radials. The student will also demonstrate the capability to promptly recover from unusual attitudes solely by reference to instruments.

Practical Test Standards

VII: Navigation

   D. Lost Procedures

IX: Basic Instrument Maneuvers

   F. Radio Communications, Navigation Systems/Facilities, and Radar Services

Date of completion _____ Time flown _____

Instructor signature _____ Student initials _____

Flight Lesson 11

Dual 0.5 Hour
Solo 0.5 Hour
Pre/Postflight 0.5 Hour

Objectives

During the dual portion of this lesson the flight instructor will introduce maximum performance takeoffs and landings. The solo portion will build student confidence in his/her ability to depart the traffic pattern, fly solo in the local training area, re-enter the traffic pattern, and land without assistance.

Content

1. Preflight discussion
2. Review
   a. Departure procedures
   b. Flight training area
   c. Traffic pattern entry
   d. No-radio airport procedures
   e. Takeoffs and landings
3. Introduction
   a. Maximum performance takeoffs and landings
      (1) Short-field takeoff and landing
      (2) Soft-field takeoff and landing
   b. Precision turns to headings (VR and IR)
      (1) Use of heading indicator vs. magnetic compass
      (2) Making small heading corrections
      (3) Maintaining altitude during turns
   c. Recovery from unusual attitudes (VR and IR)
      (1) Steep bank
      (2) Onset of climbing stall
      (3) Power-on spiral
4. Postflight critique and preview of next lesson

Completion Standards

The student will demonstrate the ability to use the magnetic compass and/or heading indicator to fly selected headings ±5 degrees. The student will also demonstrate understanding of maximum performance takeoffs and landings and be able to perform them to flight test standards.

Practical Test Standards
IX: Basic Instrument Maneuvers

   E. Recovery from Unusual Flight Attitudes

Date of completion _____ Time flown _____

Instructor signature _____ Student initials _____

Ground Lesson 6

1.5 Hours

Reading Assignment

The Complete Private Pilot, Lesson 10

Lesson Content

The VOR
VOR Orientation
Intercepting and tracking radials
VOR checks
Distance measuring equipment
The ADF
ADF Orientation
Radio Magnetic Indicator
Area Navigation
LORAN
GPS

Date of completion _____ Lesson time _____

Instructor signature _____ Student initials _____

Recommended Reading: *Private Pilot Test Prep,* Chapter 10

Flight Lesson 12

Solo 1.0 Hour (Lesson may be conducted Dual at the instructor's discretion)
Pre/Postflight 0.5 Hour

Objectives

During this solo period, the student will review and practice the basic and precision flight maneuvers learned previously, concentrating on those areas specified by the flight instructor.

Content

1. Preflight discussion
2. Review
    a. Maneuvering during slow flight
    b. Stalls
       (1) Power-off
       (2) Power-on
    c. Ground reference maneuvers
       (1) S-turns
       (2) Turns around a point
    d. Normal and/or crosswind landings
    e. Maneuvers specified by the flight instructor
3. Postflight critique and preview of next lesson

Completion Standards

This lesson will be complete when the student has successfully accomplished review and practice of the maneuvers specified.

Practical Test Standards

IV: Takeoffs, Landings, and Go-Arounds

   B. Crosswind Approach and Landing

VI: Ground Reference Maneuvers

   B. S-Turns
   C. Turns Around a Point

Date of completion _____ Time flown _____

Instructor signature _____ Student initials _____

Alternate Airport Endorsement

Instructor Note: Follow the format below when signing-off the endorsement for your students. (From AC 61-65D)

Endorsement for solo landings and takeoffs at another airport within 25 NM: 14 CFR § 61.93(a)

I have flown with Mr./Ms. _____ and find him/her competent and proficient to practice landings and takeoffs at _____ (airport name). Landings and takeoffs at _____ (airport name) are authorized subject to the following conditions: _____ (list applicable conditions).

[date]   J. Jones   654321 CFI   [expiration date]

Flight Lesson 13

Solo 1.5 Hours
Pre/Postflight 0.5 Hour

Objectives

During this lesson the student will review and practice the basic and precision flight maneuvers and maximum performance takeoffs and landings learned previously, concentrating on those areas specified by the instructor.

Content

1. Preflight discussion
2. Review
    a. Maneuvering during slow flight
    b. Stalls
    c. Steep turns
    d. Maximum performance takeoffs and landings
    e. Maneuvers specified by the flight instructor
3. Postflight critique and preview of next lesson

Completion Standards

This lesson will be complete when the student has successfully accomplished solo review and practice of the maneuvers specified.

Practical Test Standards
IV: Takeoffs, Landings, and Go-Arounds
  A. Crosswind Takeoff and Climb
  C. Soft-Field Takeoff and Climb
  D. Soft-Field Approach and Landing
  E. Short-Field Takeoff and Maximum Performance Climb
  F. Short-Field Approach and Landing

VII: Navigation
  A. Pilotage and Dead Reckoning
  B. Navigation Systems and Radar Services

VIII: Slow Flight and Stalls
  B. Power-Off Stalls
  C. Power-On Stalls
  D. Spin Awareness

Date of completion _____ Time flown _____

Instructor signature _____ Student initials _____

Ground Lesson 7

1.5 Hours

Reading Assignment
The Complete Private Pilot, Lesson 11

Lesson Content
VHF advantages and limitations
Frequency utilization
Radio procedure
Communication at controlled airports
Communication at uncontrolled airports
Transponder use
Radar services for VFR pilots
VHF/DF
Emergency communications
ELT

Date of completion _____ Lesson time _____

Instructor signature _____ Student initials _____

Recommended Reading: *Private Pilot Test Prep,* Chapter 5

Flight Lesson 14

Solo 1.0 Hour (Lesson may be conducted Dual at the instructor's discretion)
Pre/Postflight 0.5 Hour

Objectives

During this lesson the student will reinforce the basic attitude flying and navigational skills introduced in Lesson 11 by planning and flying a short (more than 25 nautical miles) cross-country flight.

Content

1. Preflight discussion
    a. Cockpit organizations and cross-country planning log
2. Review and practice
    a. Climbs
    b. Straight and level
    c. Descents
    d. Local area departure and arrival
3. Introduction
    a. VOR navigation with varying crosswind (VR)
    b. Dead reckoning
    c. Pilotage
    d. VOR failure
    e. Fuel management
    f. Unfamiliar airport operations (airplane only)
4. Postflight critique and preview of next lesson

Completion Standards

The student should demonstrate the ability to carry out a short cross-country flight by use of both visual and VOR navigation, and exhibit readiness for more ambitious trips. Aircraft should be controlled within ±200 feet in altitude and ±10° in heading.

Practical Test Standards

X: Emergency Operations

    B. Systems and Equipment Malfunctions

Date of completion _____ Time flown _____

Instructor signature _____ Student initials _____

Flight Lesson 15

Dual 1.0 Hour (0.25 Hour Instrument)
Pre/Postflight 0.5 Hour

Objectives

The student will demonstrate the ability to completely plan a cross-country flight, depart and get established on course, and compute ETAs and fuel consumption. The student will brief the instructor on Class B/Class C airspace operations or other special procedures. En route, the instructor will direct the student to simulate an encounter with adverse weather and divert to the nearest suitable airport. The student should demonstrate the ability to handle this and other emergencies, and to safely conduct cross-country flights.

Content

1. Preflight discussion and preparations

    a. Weather analysis and NOTAMs
    b. Flight planning log
    c. AIM and A/FD
    d. Aircraft performance
    e. FAA flight plan

2. Review and practice

    a. Pilotage, dead reckoning, and radio navigation
    b. Estimates and fuel consumption
    c. Departure and enroute procedures

3. Introduction

    a. Transition from visual to instrument reference
    b. Determining position by VOR
    c. Emergency determination of course to alternate
    d. Low fuel state
    e. Electrical failure
    f. VHF/DF procedures
    g. Imminent forced landing

4. Postflight critique and preview of next lesson

Completion Standards

The student should display competence in planning and flying cross-country flights, including weather analysis, alternative plans of action, and calculation of estimates and fuel consumption. Aircraft control tolerances are ±200 feet of altitude, ±10° in heading, and ±2 miles of the planned course. The student should demonstrate the ability to handle in-flight emergencies, obtain assistance, and evaluate and avoid circumstances which might lead to emergency action.

Practical Test Standards
VII: Navigation

  C. Diversion

Date of completion _____ Time flown _____

Instructor signature _____ Student initials _____

Ground Lesson 8

1.5 Hour

Reading Assignment
The Complete Private Pilot, Lesson 5

Lesson Content
Runway markings
Wind indicators
Traffic patterns
VASI
Taxiing
Crosswind operations
Wake turbulence avoidance
Line signals
Uncontrolled airports
Controlled airports
Light gun signals
National Airspace System
Airport signage

Date of completion _____ Lesson time _____

Instructor signature _____ Student initials _____

Recommended Reading: *Private Pilot Test Prep,* Chapter 11

Flight Lesson 16

Dual 1.0 Hour (0.25 Instrument, 1.0 Hour Cross-Country)
Pre/Postflight 1.0 Hour

Objectives

The student will learn to navigate over a cross-country course of more than 50 miles one way and with more than one leg, using pilotage, dead reckoning, and radio aids; will be able to compute fuel consumption and estimate times to checkpoints and destinations; file, open, and close a flight plan; operate and communicate at controlled airports; and retain orientation in unfamiliar situations.

Content

1. Preflight discussion and preparation
   a. Weather analysis and NOTAMs
   b. Cross-country planning log
   c. AIM and A/FD
   d. Class C, Class B airspace; VFR flyways
   e. Aircraft performance
   f. The FAA flight plan form
   g. Weight and balance calculations

2. Introduction
   a. Pilotage
   b. Dead reckoning
   c. VOR navigation on and off airways
   d. Radar services for VFR pilots
   e. Computing estimates and fuel consumption
   f. Departure and opening flight plan
   g. Enroute procedures; obtaining weather enroute
   h. Arrival procedures; controlled and uncontrolled airports
   i. Landing at unfamiliar airports
   j. Closing flight plan
   k. Procedures when lost or disoriented

3. Postflight critique and preview of next lesson

Completion Standards

The student will demonstrate the ability to plan and fly complex routes and navigate using pilotage, dead reckoning, and radio aids; to use the radio for en route and terminal area communications; to perform fuel and ETA calculations; and to plan and execute approaches and landings at unfamiliar airports. The student will demonstrate an understanding of how weather information is obtained and analyzed.

Continued

Practical Test Standards

I: Preflight Preparation

    C. Weather Information

    D. Cross-Country Flight Planning

    E. National Airspace System

    F. Performance and Limitations

Date of completion _____ Time flown _____

Instructor signature _____ Student initials _____

Flight Lesson 17

Dual 2.0 Hours (2.0 Hours Cross-Country, 2.0 Hours Night)
Pre/Postflight 1.0 Hour

Objectives

During this lesson the student should develop the skills and judgment necessary to enable him/her to make safe night solo flights within the airport traffic pattern and conduct safe cross-country operations. The student should understand the currency requirements for night flight and perform 5 takeoffs and landings.

Content

    1. Preflight discussion

        a. Night vision and limitations

        b Fatigue and hypoxia effect on night vision

        c. Vertigo

        d. Judgment of distance and visual illusions at night

        e. Aircraft lights

        f. Airport lighting systems; pilot-controlled lighting

        g. Federal Aviation Regulations

        h. Weather considerations

    2. Review and practice

        a. Communications

        b. Traffic pattern procedures

3. Introduction
    a. Night preflight
    b. Cockpit and position lights
    c. Anticollision lighting systems
    d. Taxiing
    e. Takeoff, climb, and area departure
    f. Area orientation
    g. Interpretation of aircraft and airport lights
    h. Emergency landings and route selection; minimum safe altitude
    i. Visual illusions and vertigo
    j. Pilotage, dead reckoning, and cross-country operations (plan a cross-country greater than 100 NM, with 3 takeoffs and landings at a tower-controlled airport)
    k. Traffic pattern entry
    l. Takeoffs and landings
        (1) Power approaches and landings
        (2) Effects of flaps on approach slope
        (3) Electrical failure—landing without lights
        (4) Five night takeoffs and landings
4. Postflight critique and preview of next lesson

Completion Standards

This lesson will be complete when the student demonstrates the ability to maintain orientation in the local flying area and traffic pattern, can accurately interpret aircraft and airport lights, can conduct safe cross-country operations, and can competently take off, fly the traffic pattern, and land at night. The student should display an understanding of emergency procedures and of preflight and pre-takeoff considerations peculiar to night operations.

Practical Test Standards

I: Preflight Preparation

    J. Aeromedical Factors

XI: Night Operation

    Night Preparation

Date of completion _____ Time flown _____

Instructor signature _____ Student initials _____

Ground Lesson 9

1.5 Hours
Stage 2 Exam

Reading Assignment

The Complete Private Pilot, Lessons 6 and 7

Lesson Content

Pressure systems
Circulation patterns
Temperature vs. moisture content
Relative humidity and dew point
Fronts: cold, warm, occluded, stationary
Stability
Cloud families
Thunderstorms
Wind shear and turbulence
Fog
Structural icing and frost
Sources of weather information
Weather reports and forecasts
METAR
Area forecasts
Terminal Aerodrome Forecasts (TAFs)
Winds aloft forecasts
Inflight advisories: AIRMETs, SIGMETs, PIREPs
Weather charts
Surface analysis
Weather depiction
Radar summary
Low-level significant weather prognostics

Date of completion _____ Lesson time _____

Instructor signature _____ Student initials _____

Recommended Reading: *Private Pilot Test Prep,* Chapter 6

Flight Lesson 18

Solo 2.5 Hours (2.5 Hours Cross-Country)
Pre/Postflight 1.0 Hour

Objectives

During this lesson the student will conduct a solo cross-country flight using pilotage, dead reckoning and radio navigation. The flight will follow the same route as Lesson 17 and include 3 takeoffs and landings at a tower-controlled airport.

Content

1. Preflight discussion
2. Preparation and instructor endorsement
3. Flight
4. Postflight critique and preview of next lesson

Completion Standards

The lesson is complete when the student has performed the solo cross-country flight and the postflight critique indicates satisfactory performance.

Date of completion _____ Time flown _____

Instructor signature _____ Student initials _____

Cross-Country Endorsements

Instructor Note: Follow the format below when signing-off the endorsement for your students (from AC 61-65D). Instructor needs to endorse the student pilot certificate also, stating category only.

1. **Endorsement for each solo cross-country flight: 14 CFR § 61.93(d)(2)(i)**

   I have reviewed the preflight planning and preparations of Mr./Ms. _____ and attest that he/she is prepared to make the solo flight safely under the known circumstances from _____ (location) to _____ (destination) via _____ (route of flight) with landings at _____ (names of applicable airports) in a _____ (make and model aircraft) on _____ (date).

   [date]   J. Jones   654321 CFI   [expiration date]

2. **Endorsement for repeated solo cross-country flights not more than 50 NM from the point of departure: 14 CFR § 61.93(d)(2)(ii)**

   I have given Mr./Ms. _____ flight instruction in both directions over the route between _____ (airport name) and _____ (airport name), including takeoffs and landings at the airports to be used, and find him/her competent to conduct repeated solo cross-country flights over that route, subject to the following conditions: _____ (list applicable conditions).

   [date]   J. Jones   654321 CFI   [expiration date]

Flight Lesson 19: Stage Check

Dual 1.0 Hour (0.25 Hour Instrument, 1.0 Hour Night)
Pre/Postflight 0.5 Hour

Objectives

To confirm that the student can plan and conduct a cross-country flight including a diversion to an alternate airport as necessary to avoid adverse weather and conduct safe night operations. This stage check will be conducted by the Chief Flight Instructor or the Assistant Chief Flight Instructor. Include 5 takeoffs and landings.

Content

1. Preparation—the student will plan a round-robin cross-country flight including at least one controlled airport (if available).
2. Evaluation—planning, filing, flying, navigation, diversions and emergencies will be covered.
3. Postflight critique

Completion Standards

The student will demonstrate the ability to safely conduct cross-country flight operations and demonstrate a thorough knowledge of proper preflight action, flight planning, weather analysis, flight planning publications, and night operations. All pilot duties will be performed with smoothness, accuracy, and competence. The student should be able to divert to an alternate airport and give a reasonable estimate of arrival time and remaining fuel. The student should be able to use VOR for orientation, fixing the airplane's position within three miles. The student will be able to:

1. Establish and maintain headings required to stay on course
2. Correctly fix his/her position at any time
3. Provide estimates with an error of not more than ten minutes
4. Maintain altitude within ±200 feet
5. Establish a course to an alternate and give a reasonable estimate of time and fuel required to reach the alternate.

Date of completion _____ Time flown _____

Instructor signature _____ Student initials _____

Stage 3: Pilot Operations

Flight Training

4.5 Hours Dual (0.75 Hour Instrument)
8.0 Hours Solo (8.0 hours may be conducted Dual at the instructor's discretion)
(7.0 hours cross-country; all of which may be conducted Dual at the Instructor's discretion)

Objectives

The student will gain further experience in cross-country practice and receive instruction in preparation for the private pilot flight test.

Completion Standards

This stage will be completed when the student satisfactorily passes the final stage check for the course and meets all the flight time requirements set forth in 14 CFR Part 141 or Part 61.

Ground Training

10.0 Hours
Stage 3 Exam
Final Exam

Objective

In Stage 3, the student will learn where to find information vital to safe flight, and learn how flight affects pilots physiologically. A review of pertinent Federal Aviation Regulations and a typical cross-country flight complete Stage 3.

Completion Standards

Stage 3 will be complete when the student has passed the Stage 3 written examination with a passing grade of 80 percent or better, and has reviewed, with the instructor, subject areas in which the student is weak.

Ground Lesson 10

1.5 Hours

Reading Assignment
The Complete Private Pilot, Lessons 4 and 5

Lesson Content
Aeronautical Information Manual (AIM)
Pilot/Controller Glossary
Federal Aviation Regulations
Airport/Facility Directory (A/FD)
Advisory Circulars (ACs)
Notices to Airmen
Drugs and alcohol
Hypoxia and hyperventilation
Carbon monoxide poisoning
Ear problems
Vertigo
Night vision and scanning
Aeronautical decision-making
Judgement

Date of completion _____ Lesson time _____

Instructor signature _____ Student initials _____

Recommended Reading: *Private Pilot Test Prep,* Chapter 7

Flight Lesson 20

Solo 3.0 Hours (3.0 Hours Cross-Country; lesson may be conducted Dual at the instructor's discretion)
Pre/Postflight 1.0 Hour

Objectives

During this lesson the student will conduct a three-leg solo cross-country flight. Practice at locating small airports will be gained en route, with an optional landing if conditions permit.

Content

1. Preflight discussion

    a. Class B/Class C airspace considerations
    b. Special use airspace
    c. Hills/mountainous terrain considerations
    d. Route selection
    e. Selection of cruising altitude

2. Preparation

3. Flight. At least one leg will be flown using pilotage and dead reckoning only, if feasible. The student will attempt to locate and identify airports en route, and may elect to land at an airport designated by the instructor if conditions permit. The student should obtain logbook entries at each point of landing, if possible.

4. Postflight critique and preview of next lesson

Completion Standards

The student will have completed a solo cross-country with designated stops. The instructor will debrief the student to determine how well the flight was conducted.

Date of completion _____ Time flown _____

Instructor signature _____ Student initials _____

Flight Lesson 21

Solo 4.0 Hours (4.0 Hours Cross-Country; lesson may be conducted Dual at the instructor's discretion)
Pre/Postflight 1.0 Hour

Objectives

During this lesson the student will conduct a three-leg solo cross-country flight totaling at least 300 NM. One landing shall be made at an airport at least 100 NM from the original departure point.

Content

1. Preflight discussion
2. Preparation
    a. Obtaining weather reports and forecasts
    b. Updating weather information in flight
3. Flight
    a. Student should obtain logbook entries at each point of landing, if possible.
4. Postflight critique and preview of next lesson

Completion Standards

The student will complete a long cross-country flight. The instructor will debrief the student to determine how well the flight was conducted.

Date of completion _____ Time flown _____

Instructor signature _____ Student initials _____

Ground Lesson 11

1.5 Hours

Reading Assignment
The Complete Private Pilot, Lesson 4

Lesson Content
14 CFR Part 61
14 CFR Part 91
NTSB Part 830

Date of completion _____ Lesson time _____

Instructor signature _____ Student initials _____

Recommended Reading: *Private Pilot Test Prep,* Chapter 4

Flight Lesson 22

Dual 1.5 Hours (0.25 Instrument)
Pre/Postflight 0.5 Hour

Objectives
The student will be able to perform advanced maneuvers which were previously introduced.

Content
1. Preflight discussion
2. Review
   a. Short-field takeoffs and landings
   b. Soft-field takeoffs and landings
   c. Ground reference maneuvers
   d. Maneuvering during slow flight
   e. Stalls
   f. Steep turns

Continued

g. Maneuvering by reference to flight instruments

h. Emergency operations

i. Maximum performance takeoffs and landings

3. Postflight critique and preview of next lesson

Completion Standards

The student should demonstrate proficiency in all advanced maneuvers and exercise pilot-in-command responsibility and judgment in all operations.

Date of completion _____ Time flown _____

Instructor signature _____ Student initials _____

Flight Lesson 23

Solo 1.0 Hour (Lesson may be conducted Dual at the instructor's discretion)
Pre/Postflight 1.0 Hour

Objectives

The student will be able to perform specific flight maneuvers assigned by the flight instructor to increase proficiency.

Content

1. Preflight discussion

2. Performance of assigned maneuvers

3. Postflight critique and preview of next lesson

Completion Standards

The student has completed the specific flight maneuvers assigned by the flight instructor.

Date of completion _____ Time flown _____

Instructor signature _____ Student initials _____

Ground Lesson 12

1.5 Hours
Stage Exam

Reading Assignment
The Complete Private Pilot, Lesson 11

Lesson Content
Filing a flight plan
Preparing a flight log
The cross-country flight

Date of completion _____ Lesson time _____

Instructor signature _____ Student initials _____

Stage exam score _____

Flight Lesson 24: Stage Check

Dual 1.5 Hours (0.25 Instrument)
Pre/Postflight 1.0 Hour

Objectives
The student will be able to demonstrate the required preparation and proficiency in the practical test for a private pilot certificate. This stage check will be conducted by the Chief Flight Instructor or assistant.

Content
1. Preflight discussion and oral examination
2. Review of maneuvers specified in the Private Pilot Practical Test Standards
3. Postflight critique

Continued

Completion Standards

The student will demonstrate proficiency in the practical test for a private pilot certificate with all maneuvers accomplished promptly, without assistance, and to the tolerances specified in the Practical Test Standards. The student will display pilot-in-command responsibility, knowledge, and judgment throughout. Any time there is a necessity for the instructor to assume command or control, this will be disqualifying. A graduation certificate will be issued upon satisfactory completion.

Date of completion _____ Time flown _____

Instructor signature _____ Student initials _____

Stage check successful _____

Flight Lesson 25

Dual 1.5 Hours (0.25 Instrument)
Pre/Postflight 1.0 Hour

Objectives

During this lesson the instructor will determine the student's proficiency in all maneuvers and procedures necessary to conduct flight operations as a private pilot.

Content

1. Preflight discussion and oral examination
2. Review of previously covered procedures and maneuvers

Completion Standards

The student should display the ability to meet the requirements of the Private Pilot Practical Test Standards for operations as a private pilot.

Date of completion _____ Time flown _____

Instructor signature _____ Student initials _____

Private Pilot Endorsements

Instructor Note: Follow the formats below when signing-off endorsements for your students (from AC 61-65D).

1. Endorsement for aeronautical knowledge: 14 CFR § 61.35(a)(1) and 61.105(a)

I certify that I have given Mr./Ms. _____ the ground instruction required by
14 CFR § 61.105(a)(1) through (5).

[date]   J. Jones   654321 CFI   [expiration date]

2. Endorsement for flight proficiency: 14 CFR § 61.107(a)

I certify that I have given Mr./Ms. _____ the flight instruction required by
14 CFR § 61.107(a)(1) through (10) and find him/her competent to perform each pilot operation safely as a
private pilot.

[date]   J. Jones   654321 CFI   [expiration date]

Checkride Checklist

❑ Graded pre-solo written exam

❑ Current Student Pilot certificate

❑ Each solo cross-country endorsed

❑ 90-day current solo endorsement (if necessary)

❑ Student certificate endorsed by instructor

❑ Application form (8710-1) filled out completely

❑ Logbook and necessary supplies readily accessible

❑ Materials necessary for planning a cross-country flight

❑ FAA Knowledge Exam results

❑ Identification with photo and signature

❑ Instructor endorsements for checkride

❑ Graduation certificate

❑ Examiner's fee

❑ Current Medical

Pre-Solo Exam

1. If the outside air temperature (OAT) at a given altitude is warmer than standard, the density altitude is

   A—equal to pressure altitude.
   B—lower than pressure altitude.
   C—higher than pressure altitude.

2. Which combination of atmospheric conditions will reduce aircraft takeoff and climb performance?

   A—Low temperature, low relative humidity, and low density altitude.
   B—High temperature, low relative humidity, and low density altitude.
   C—High temperature, high relative humidity, and high density altitude.

3. If the temperature/dew point spread is small and decreasing, and the temperature is 62°F, what type of weather is most likely to develop?

   A—Freezing precipitation.
   B—Thunderstorms.
   C—Fog or low clouds.

4. Which type of weather briefing should a pilot request, when departing within the hour, if no preliminary weather information has been received?

   A—An outlook briefing.
   B—An abbreviated briefing.
   C—A standard briefing.

5. What conditions are necessary for the formation of thunderstorms?

   A—High humidity, lifting force, and unstable conditions.
   B—High humidity, high temperature, and cumulus clouds.
   C—Lifting force, moist air, and extensive cloud cover.

6. When telephoning a weather briefing facility for preflight weather information, pilots should state

   A—the full name and address of the pilot-in-command.
   B—the intended route, destination, and type of aircraft.
   C—the radio frequencies to be used.

7. Who is responsible for making the go-no go decision for each flight?

   A—Pilot-in-command.
   B—Certified flight instructor.
   C—Chief flight instructor.

8. What information is necessary in order to make a go-no go decision?

   A—Permission from the chief flight instructor, chief mechanic, and weather briefer.
   B—Acceptable weather conditions, an airworthy aircraft, and an airworthy pilot.
   C—Permission from the weather briefer, an airworthy aircraft, and an airworthy pilot.

9. Two-way radio communication must be established with the Air Traffic Control facility having jurisdiction over the area prior to entering which class airspace?

   A—Class C.
   B—Class E.
   C—Class G.

10. Unless otherwise authorized, two-way radio communications with Air Traffic Control are required for landings and takeoffs

    A—at all tower controlled airports within Class D airspace only when weather conditions are less than VFR.
    B—at all tower controlled airports regardless of weather conditions.
    C—at all tower controlled airports only when weather conditions are less than VFR.

11. Which is the correct traffic pattern departure procedure to use at a noncontrolled airport?

A—Comply with any FAA traffic pattern established for the airport.

B—Depart in any direction consistent with safety, after crossing the airport boundary.

C—Make all turns to the left.

12. An airport's rotating beacon operated during daylight hours indicates

A—that weather at the airport located in Class D airspace is below basic VFR weather minimums.

B—there are obstructions on the airport.

C—the Air Traffic Control tower is not in operation.

13. The official source of sunrise and sunset times is

A—the Aeronautical Information Manual.

B—the American Air Almanac.

C—the Federal Aviation Regulations.

14. An aircraft departs an airport in the Eastern Daylight Time Zone at 0945 EDT for a 2-hour flight to an airport located in the Central Daylight Time Zone. The landing should be at what coordinated universal time?

A—1345Z.

B—1445Z.

C—1545Z.

15. In order to comply with Private Practical Test Standards, students must perform Turns Around a Point and S-turns

A—at traffic pattern altitude, while maintaining altitude ±100 feet, and airspeed ±10 knots, while maintaining coordination.

B—between 600 and 1,000 feet AGL, while maintaining altitude ±100 feet, and airspeed ±10 knots, while maintaining coordination.

C—at traffic pattern altitude, while maintaining altitude ±100 feet, and heading ±10 degrees, while maintaining coordination.

16. In order to comply with Private Practical Test Standards, the student must perform Rectangular Course

A—between 600 and 1,000 feet AGL, while maintaining altitude ±100 feet, and airspeed ±10 knots, while maintaining coordination.

B—between 600 and 1,000 feet AGL, entering 45° to the downwind, while maintaining coordination.

C—at traffic pattern altitude, while maintaining altitude ±100 feet, and airspeed ±10 knots, while maintaining coordination.

17. In headwind conditions, the groundspeed will _____ the airspeed.

A—exceed

B—be less than

C—be the same as

18. To maintain a desired track over the ground, apply

A—a wind correction angle into the wind.

B—a wind correction angle out of the wind.

C—power and a steeper bank angle.

19. The numbers 9 and 27 on a runway indicate that the runway is oriented approximately

A—009° and 027° true.

B—090° and 270° true.

C—090° and 270° magnetic.

20. If two-way communication fails at an airport with a tower and cannot be restored, the recommended procedure is to

A—make an off-airport landing.

B—turn on your landing light, enter the airport area on final approach, and land as soon as possible.

C—observe traffic flow, enter the traffic pattern on the downwind, look for light signals from the tower, and squawk 7600 on your transponder.

21. In an in-flight emergency requiring emergency action, the pilot-in-command

A—may deviate from any rule of FAR Part 91 to the extent required to meet that emergency.

B—must not deviate from any rule of FAR Part 91.

C—may deviate from any rule of FAR Part 91 but only after receiving prior permission from ATC.

22. When approaching another aircraft head-on, each pilot must alter his/her course

A—to the left.
B—to the right.
C—with a descent.

23. Normal and crosswind takeoffs and landings should take place

A—with the wind.
B—into the wind.
C—perpendicular to the wind.

24. When you fly solo, you are pilot-in-command, and you are required to have in your personal possession a

A—pilot certificate and logbook.
B—pilot certificate and medicate certificate.
C—CFI solo endorsement, and copy of the FAR/AIM.

25. Student pilots are responsible for all information, rules, and regulations in FAR Parts

A—61, and 91.
B—91, and 121.
C—1, and 67.

26. A person may not act as a crewmember of a civil aircraft if alcoholic beverages have been consumed by that person within the preceding

A—8 hours.
B—12 hours.
C—24 hours.

27. List the airspeeds and their definitions, for the training aircraft to be used for solo flight:

	Speed	Definition
Short-field takeoff	___	_____
Short-field landing	___	_____
Normal takeoff	___	_____
Normal landing	___	_____
Soft-field takeoff	___	_____
Soft-field landing	___	_____
To practice Private maneuvers	___	_____
V_{S1}	___	_____
V_{S0}	___	_____
V_A	___	_____
V_X	___	_____
V_Y	___	_____
V_{FE}	___	_____
V_{NO}	___	_____
V_{NE}	___	_____
Best Glide	___	_____

28. List the grade and capacity of the fuel and oil to be used in the training aircraft used for solo flight:

	Grade	Capacity
Fuel	_____	_____
Oil	_____	_____

29. What do each of the following ATC light signals mean?

	In Flight	On the Ground
Steady green	_____	_____
Flashing green	_____	_____
Steady red	_____	_____
Flashing red	_____	_____
Flashing white	_____	_____
Alternating red and green	_____	_____

30. What actions will you take for an engine failure:

Right after takeoff _____

_____

50 feet after takeoff _____

_____

Downwind, in the traffic pattern _____

_____

In the practice area _____

_____

Stage 1 Exam

1. What is true altitude?

   A—The vertical distance of the aircraft above sea level.

   B—The vertical distance of the aircraft above the surface.

   C—The height above the standard datum plane.

2. What is pressure altitude?

   A—The indicated altitude corrected for position and installation error.

   B—The altitude indicated when the barometric pressure scale is set to 29.92.

   C—The indicated altitude corrected for nonstandard temperature and pressure.

3. Under what condition is indicated altitude the same as true altitude?

   A—If the altimeter has no mechanical error.

   B—When at sea level under standard conditions.

   C—When at 18,000 feet MSL with the altimeter set at 29.92.

4. Under what condition will true altitude be lower than indicated altitude?

   A—In colder than standard air temperature.

   B—In warmer than standard air temperature.

   C—When density altitude is higher than indicated altitude.

5. If it is necessary to set the altimeter from 29.15 to 29.85, what change occurs?

   A—70-foot increase in indicated altitude.

   B—70-foot increase in density altitude.

   C—700-foot increase in indicated altitude.

6. With regard to carburetor ice, float-type carburetor systems in comparison to fuel injection systems are generally considered to be

   A—more susceptible to icing.

   B—equally susceptible to icing.

   C—susceptible to icing only when visible moisture is present.

7. The presence of carburetor ice in an aircraft equipped with a fixed-pitch propeller can be verified by applying carburetor heat and noting

   A—an increase in RPM and then a gradual decrease in RPM.

   B—a decrease in RPM and then a constant RPM indication.

   C—a decrease in RPM and then a gradual increase in RPM.

8. What change occurs in the fuel/air mixture when carburetor heat is applied?

   A—A decrease in RPM results from the lean mixture.

   B—The fuel/air mixture becomes richer.

   C—The fuel/air mixture becomes leaner.

9. Generally speaking, the use of carburetor heat tends to

   A—decrease engine performance.

   B—increase engine performance.

   C—have no effect on engine performance.

10. One purpose of the dual ignition system on an aircraft engine is to provide for

    A—improved engine performance.

    B—uniform heat distribution.

    C—balanced cylinder head pressure.

11. For internal cooling, reciprocating aircraft engines are especially dependent on

    A—a properly functioning thermostat.

    B—air flowing over the exhaust manifold.

    C—the circulation of lubricating oil.

12. If the engine oil temperature and cylinder head temperature gauges have exceeded their normal operating range, the pilot may have been operating with

A—the mixture set too rich.

B—higher-than-normal oil pressure.

C—too much power and with the mixture set too lean.

13. Detonation occurs in a reciprocating aircraft engine when

A—the spark plugs are fouled or shorted out or the wiring is defective.

B—hot spots in the combustion chamber ignite the fuel/air mixture in advance of normal ignition.

C—the unburned charge in the cylinders explodes instead of burning normally.

14. On aircraft equipped with fuel pumps, the practice of running a fuel tank dry before switching tanks is considered unwise because

A—the engine-driven fuel pump or electric fuel boost pump may draw air into the fuel system and cause vapor lock.

B—the engine-driven fuel pump is lubricated by fuel and operating on a dry tank may cause pump failure.

C—any foreign matter in the tank will be pumped into the fuel system.

15. What type fuel can be substituted for an aircraft if the recommended octane is not available?

A—The next higher octane aviation gas.

B—The next lower octane aviation gas.

C—Unleaded automotive gas of the same octane rating.

16. The basic purpose of adjusting the fuel/air mixture at altitude is to

A—decrease the amount of fuel in the mixture in order to compensate for increased air density.

B—decrease the fuel flow in order to compensate for decreased air density.

C—increase the amount of fuel in the mixture to compensate for the decrease in pressure and density of the air.

17. (Refer to Figure 1-1.) How should a pilot determine the direction of bank from an attitude indicator such as the one illustrated?

A—By the direction of deflection of the banking scale (A).

B—By the direction of deflection of the horizon bar (B).

C—By the relationship of the miniature airplane (C) to the deflected horizon bar (B).

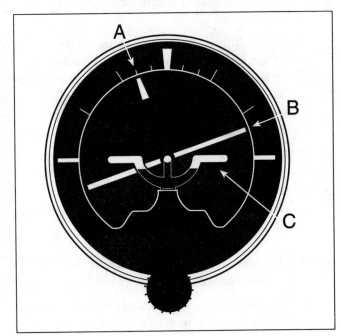

Figure 1-1

18. (Refer to Figure 1-2.) To receive accurate indications during flight from a heading indicator, the instrument must be

A—set prior to flight on a known heading.
B—calibrated on a compass rose at regular intervals.
C—periodically realigned with the magnetic compass as the gyro precesses.

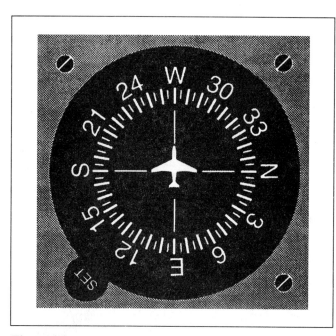

Figure 1-2

19. In the Northern Hemisphere, if an aircraft is accelerated or decelerated, the magnetic compass will normally indicate

A—a turn momentarily.
B—correctly when on a north or south heading.
C—a turn toward the south.

20. Deviation in a magnetic compass is caused by the

A—presence of flaws in the permanent magnets of the compass.
B—difference in the location between true north and magnetic north.
C—magnetic fields within the aircraft distorting the lines of magnetic force.

21. (Refer to Figure 1-3.) What is the full flap operating range for the airplane?

A—60 to 100 MPH.
B—60 to 208 MPH.
C—65 to 165 MPH.

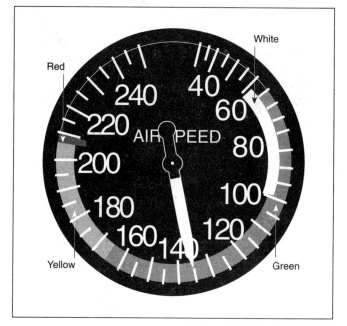

Figure 1-3

22. The pitot system provides impact pressure for which instrument?

A—Altimeter.
B—Vertical-speed indicator.
C—Airspeed indicator.

23. (Refer to Figure 1-3.) What is the maximum flaps-extended speed?

A—65 MPH.
B—100 MPH.
C—165 MPH.

24. (Refer to Figure 1-4). Altimeter 1 indicates

A—500 feet.
B—1,500 feet.
C—10,500 feet.

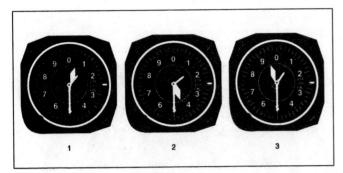

Figure 1-4

25. Which instrument will become inoperative if the pitot tube becomes clogged?

A—Altimeter.
B—Vertical speed.
C—Airspeed.

26. When are the four forces that act on an airplane in equilibrium?

A—During unaccelerated flight.
B—When the aircraft is accelerating.
C—When the aircraft is at rest on the ground.

27. One of the main functions of flaps during approach and landing is to

A—decrease the angle of descent without increasing the airspeed.
B—permit a touchdown at a higher indicated airspeed.
C—increase the angle of descent without increasing the airspeed.

28. The term "angle of attack" is defined as the angle

A—between the wing chord line and the relative wind.
B—between the airplane's climb angle and the horizon.
C—formed by the longitudinal axis of the airplane and the chord line of the wing.

29. (Refer to Figure 1-5.) If an airplane weighs 3,300 pounds, what approximate weight would the airplane structure be required to support during a 30° banked turn while maintaining altitude?

A—1,200 pounds.
B—3,100 pounds.
C—3,960 pounds.

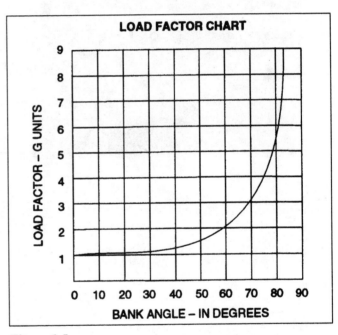

Figure 1-5

30. The left turning tendency of an airplane caused by P-factor is the result of the

A—clockwise rotation of the engine and the propeller turning the airplane counterclockwise.

B—propeller blade descending on the right, producing more thrust than the ascending blade on the left.

C—gyroscopic forces applied to the rotating propeller blades acting 90° in advance of the point the force was applied.

31. Which basic flight maneuver increases the load factor on an airplane as compared to straight-and-level flight?

A—Climbs.

B—Turns.

C—Stalls.

32. What determines the longitudinal stability of an airplane?

A—The location of the CG with respect to the center of lift.

B—The effectiveness of the horizontal stabilizer, rudder, and rudder trim tab.

C—The relationship of thrust and lift to weight and drag.

33. What causes an airplane (except a T-tail) to pitch nosedown when power is reduced and controls are not adjusted?

A—The CG shifts forward when thrust and drag are reduced.

B—The downwash on the elevators from the propeller slipstream is reduced and elevator effectiveness is reduced.

C—When thrust is reduced to less than weight, lift is also reduced and the wings can no longer support the weight.

34. Loading an airplane to the most aft CG will cause the airplane to be

A—less stable at all speeds.

B—less stable at slow speeds, but more stable at high speeds.

C—less stable at high speeds, but more stable at low speeds.

35. As altitude increases, the indicated airspeed at which a given airplane stalls in a particular configuration will

A—decrease as the true airspeed decreases.

B—decrease as the true airspeed increases.

C—remain the same regardless of altitude.

36. In what flight condition must an aircraft be placed in order to spin?

A—Partially stalled with one wing low.

B—In a steep diving spiral.

C—Stalled.

37. An aircraft is loaded 110 pounds over maximum certificated gross weight. If fuel (gasoline) is drained to bring the aircraft weight within limits, how much fuel should be drained?

A—15.7 gallons.

B—16.2 gallons.

C—18.4 gallons.

38. (Refer to Figure 1-6.) What is the maximum amount of baggage that may be loaded aboard the airplane for the CG to remain within the moment envelope?

	WEIGHT (LB)	MOM/1000
Empty weight	1,350	51.5
Pilot and front passenger	250	—
Rear passengers	400	—
Baggage	—	—
Fuel, 30 gal	—	—
Oil, 8 qt	—	-0.2

A—105 pounds.
B—110 pounds.
C—120 pounds.

39. Determine the moment/1000 with the following data using the graphs in Figure 1-6.

	WEIGHT (LB)	MOM/1000
Empty weight	1,350	51.5
Pilot and front passenger	340	—
Fuel, (std tanks)	Capacity	—
Oil, 8 qt	—	—

A—69.9 lb.-in.
B—74.9 lb.-in.
C—77.6 lb.-in.

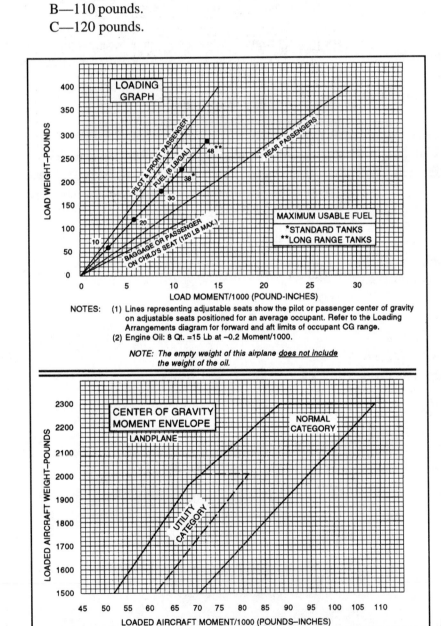

Figure 1-6

40. (Refer to Figures 1-7 and 1-8.) Determine if the airplane weight and balance is within limits.

Front seat occupants .... 340 lb
Rear seat occupants .... 295 lb
Fuel, main tanks .... 44 gal
Baggage .... 56 lb

A—20 pounds overweight, CG aft of aft limits.
B—20 pounds overweight, CG within limits.
C—20 pounds overweight, CG forward of forward limits.

41. How is engine operation controlled on an engine equipped with a constant-speed propeller?

A—The throttle controls power output as registered on the manifold pressure gauge and the propeller control regulates engine RPM.
B—The throttle controls power output as registered on the manifold pressure gauge and the propeller control regulates a constant blade angle.
C—The throttle controls engine RPM as registered on the tachometer and the mixture control regulates the power output.

USEFUL LOAD WEIGHTS AND MOMENTS

OCCUPANTS

FRONT SEATS ARM 85		REAR SEATS ARM 121	
Weight	Moment/100	Weight	Moment/100
120	102	120	145
130	110	130	157
140	119	140	169
150	128	150	182
160	136	160	194
170	144	170	206
180	153	180	218
190	162	190	230
200	170	200	242

BAGGAGE OR 5TH SEAT OCCUPANT ARM 140

Weight	Moment/100
10	14
20	28
30	42
40	56
50	70
60	84
70	98
80	112
90	126
100	140
110	154
120	168
130	182
140	196
150	210
160	224
170	238
180	252
190	266
200	280
210	294
220	308
230	322
240	336
250	350
260	364
270	378

USABLE FUEL

MAIN WING TANKS ARM 75

Gallons	Weight	Moment/100
5	30	22
10	60	45
15	90	68
20	120	90
25	150	112
30	180	135
35	210	158
40	240	180
44	264	198

AUXILIARY WING TANKS ARM 94

Gallons	Weight	Moment/100
5	30	28
10	60	56
15	90	85
19	114	107

*OIL

Quarts	Weight	Moment/100
10	19	5

*Included in basic Empty Weight

Empty Weight ~ 2015
MOM / 100 ~ 1554

MOMENT LIMITS vs WEIGHT

Moment limits are based on the following weight and center of gravity limit data (landing gear down).

WEIGHT CONDITION	FORWARD CG LIMIT	AFT CG LIMIT
2950 lb (takeoff or landing)	82.1	84.7
2525 lb	77.5	85.7
2475 lb or less	77.0	85.7

Figure 1-7

MOMENT LIMITS vs WEIGHT (Continued)

Weight	Minimum Moment 100	Maximum Moment 100	Weight	Minimum Moment 100	Maximum Moment 100
2100	1617	1800	2600	2037	2224
2110	1625	1808	2610	2048	2232
2120	1632	1817	2620	2058	2239
2130	1640	1825	2630	2069	2247
2140	1648	1834	2640	2080	2255
2150	1656	1843	2650	2090	2263
2160	1663	1851	2660	2101	2271
2170	1671	1860	2670	2112	2279
2180	1679	1868	2680	2123	2287
2190	1686	1877	2690	2133	2295
2200	1694	1885	2700	2144	2303
2210	1702	1894	2710	2155	2311
2220	1709	1903	2720	2166	2319
2230	1717	1911	2730	2177	2326
2240	1725	1920	2740	2188	2334
2250	1733	1928	2750	2199	2342
2260	1740	1937	2760	2210	2350
2270	1748	1945	2770	2221	2358
2280	1756	1954	2780	2232	2366
2290	1763	1963	2790	2243	2374
2300	1771	1971			
2310	1779	1980	2800	2254	2381
2320	1786	1988	2810	2265	2389
2330	1794	1997	2820	2276	2397
2340	1802	2005	2830	2287	2405
2350	1810	2014	2840	2298	2413
2360	1817	2023	2850	2309	2421
2370	1825	2031	2860	2320	2428
2380	1833	2040	2870	2332	2436
2390	1840	2048	2880	2343	2444
			2890	2354	2452
2400	1848	2057	2900	2365	2460
2410	1856	2065	2910	2377	2468
2420	1863	2074	2920	2388	2475
2430	1871	2083	2930	2399	2483
2440	1879	2091	2940	2411	2491
2450	1887	2100	2950	2422	2499
2460	1894	2108			
2470	1902	2117			
2480	1911	2125			
2490	1921	2134			
2500	1932	2143			
2510	1942	2151			
2520	1953	2160			
2530	1963	2168			
2540	1974	2176			
2550	1984	2184			
2560	1995	2192			
2570	2005	2200			
2580	2016	2208			
2590	2026	2216			

Figure 1-8

42. A precaution for the operation of an engine equipped with a constant-speed propeller is to

A—avoid high RPM settings with high manifold pressure.

B—avoid high manifold pressure settings with low RPM.

C—always use a rich mixture with high RPM settings.

43. What should be the first action after starting an aircraft engine?

A—Adjust for proper RPM and check for desired indications on the engine gauges.

B—Place the magneto or ignition switch momentarily in the OFF position to check for proper grounding.

C—Test each brake and the parking brake.

44. The most important rule to remember in the event of a power failure after becoming airborne is to

A—immediately establish the proper gliding attitude and airspeed.

B—quickly check the fuel supply for possible fuel exhaustion.

C—determine the wind direction to plan for the forced landing.

45. At what altitude shall the altimeter be set to 29.92, when climbing to cruising flight level?

A—14,500 feet MSL.

B—18,000 feet MSL.

C—24,000 feet MSL.

46. What is density altitude?

A—The height above the standard datum plane.

B—The pressure altitude corrected for nonstandard temperature.

C—The altitude read directly from the altimeter.

47. What effect does high density altitude have on aircraft performance?

A—It increases engine performance.

B—It reduces climb performance.

C—It increases takeoff performance.

48. (Refer to Figure 1-9.) What is the effect of a temperature increase from 26 to 50°F on the density altitude if the pressure altitude remains at 5,000 feet?

A—1,200-foot increase.

B—1,400-foot increase.

C—1,650-foot increase.

49. Which combination of atmospheric conditions will reduce aircraft takeoff and climb performance?

A—Low temperature, low relative humidity, and low density altitude.

B—High temperature, low relative humidity, and low density altitude.

C—High temperature, high relative humidity, and high density altitude.

50. What effect does high density altitude, as compared to low density altitude, have on propeller efficiency and why?

A—Efficiency is increased due to less friction on the propeller blades.

B—Efficiency is reduced because the propeller exerts less force at high density altitudes than at low density altitudes.

C—Efficiency is reduced due to the increased force of the propeller in the thinner air.

51. What must a pilot be aware of as a result of ground effect?

A—Wingtip vortices increase creating wake turbulence problems for arriving and departing aircraft.

B—Induced drag decreases; therefore, any excess speed at the point of flare may cause considerable floating.

C—A full stall landing will require less up elevator deflection than would a full stall when done free of ground effect.

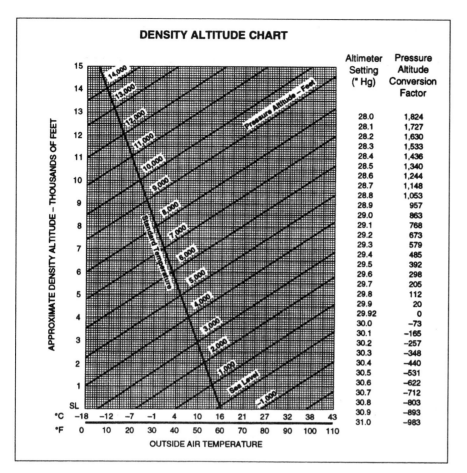

DENSITY ALTITUDE CHART

Altimeter Setting (" Hg)	Pressure Altitude Conversion Factor
28.0	1,824
28.1	1,727
28.2	1,630
28.3	1,533
28.4	1,436
28.5	1,340
28.6	1,244
28.7	1,148
28.8	1,053
28.9	957
29.0	863
29.1	768
29.2	673
29.3	579
29.4	485
29.5	392
29.6	298
29.7	205
29.8	112
29.9	20
29.92	0
30.0	−73
30.1	−165
30.2	−257
30.3	−348
30.4	−440
30.5	−531
30.6	−622
30.7	−712
30.8	−803
30.9	−893
31.0	−983

Figure 1-9

52. (Refer to Figure 1-10.) What is the expected fuel consumption for a 1,000-nautical mile flight under the following conditions?

Pressure altitude .... 8,000 ft
Temperature .... 22°C
Manifold pressure .... 20.8" Hg
Wind .... Calm

A—60.2 gallons.
B—70.1 gallons.
C—73.2 gallons.

53. (Refer to Figure 1-11.) Determine the total distance required to land.

OAT .... 32°F
Pressure altitude .... 8,000 ft
Weight .... 2,600 lb
Headwind component .... 20 kts
Obstacle .... 50 ft

A—850 feet.
B—1,400 feet.
C—1,750 feet.

54. (Refer to Figure 1-12.) Determine the total distance required for takeoff to clear a 50-foot obstacle.

OAT .... Std
Pressure altitude .... Sea level
Takeoff weight .... 2,700 lb
Headwind component .... Calm

A—1,000 feet.
B—1,400 feet.
C—1,700 feet.

Cruise Power Settings 65% Maximum Continuous Power (or Full Throttle) 2,800 lbs

Pressure Altitude Feet	ISA -20°C (-36°F)						Standard Day (ISA)						ISA +20°C (+36°F)					
	IOAT °F °C	Engine Speed RPM	Manifold Pressure IN HG	Fuel Flow Per Engine PSI GPH	TAS KTS MPH		IOAT °F °C	Engine Speed RPM	Manifold Pressure IN HG	Fuel Flow Per Engine PSI GPH	TAS KTS MPH		IOAT °F °C	Engine Speed RPM	Manifold Pressure IN HG	Fuel Flow Per Engine PSI GPH	TAS KTS MPH	
Sea Level	27 -3	2450	20.7	6.6 11.5	147 169		63 17	2450	21.2	6.6 11.5	150 173		99 37	2450	21.8	6.6 11.5	153 176	
2000	19 -7	2450	20.4	6.6 11.5	149 171		55 13	2450	21.0	6.6 11.5	153 176		91 33	2450	21.5	6.6 11.5	156 180	
4000	12 -11	2450	20.1	6.6 11.5	152 175		48 9	2450	20.7	6.6 11.5	156 180		84 29	2450	21.3	6.6 11.5	159 183	
6000	5 -5	2450	19.8	6.6 11.5	155 178		41 5	2450	20.4	6.6 11.5	158 182		79 26	2450	21.0	6.6 11.5	161 185	
8000	-2 -9	2450	19.5	6.6 11.5	157 181		36 2	2450	20.2	6.6 11.5	161 185		72 22	2450	20.8	6.6 11.5	164 189	
10,000	-8 -22	2450	19.2	6.6 11.5	160 184		28 -2	2450	19.9	6.6 11.5	163 188		64 18	2450	20.3	6.5 11.4	166 191	
12,000	-15 -26	2450	18.8	6.4 11.3	162 186		21 -8	2450	18.8	6.1 10.9	163 188		57 14	2450	18.8	5.9 10.6	163 188	
14,000	-22 -30	2450	17.4	5.8 10.5	159 183		14 -10	2450	17.4	5.6 10.1	160 184		50 10	2450	17.4	5.4 9.8	160 184	
16,000	-29 -34	2450	16.1	5.3 9.7	156 180		7 -14	2450	16.1	5.1 9.4	156 180		43 6	2450	16.1	4.9 9.1	155 178	

Notes   1. Full throttle manifold pressure settings are approximate.   2. Shaded area represents operation with full throttle.

Figure 1-10

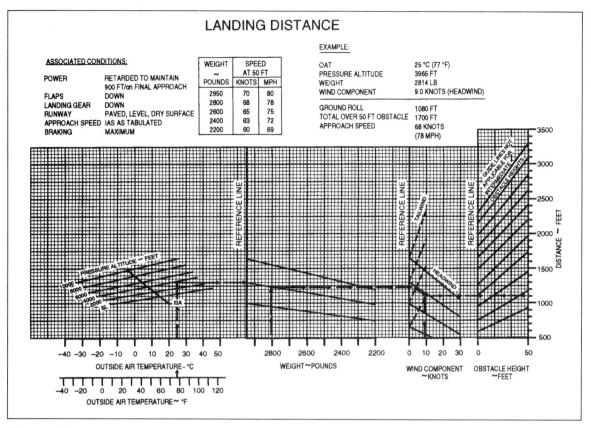

Figure 1-11

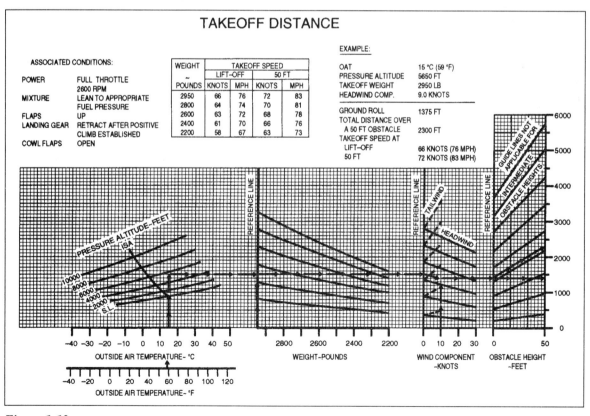

Figure 1-12

Stage 2 Exam

1. (Refer to Figure 1-9 on Page 61.) Determine the pressure altitude at an airport that is 3,563 feet MSL with an altimeter setting of 29.96.

   A—3,527 feet MSL.
   B—3,556 feet MSL.
   C—3,639 feet MSL.

2. If a pilot changes the altimeter setting from 30.11 to 29.96, what is the approximate change in indication?

   A—Altimeter will indicate .15" Hg higher.
   B—Altimeter will indicate 150 feet higher.
   C—Altimeter will indicate 150 feet lower.

3. Floating caused by the phenomenon of ground effect will be most realized during an approach to land when at

   A—less than the length of the wingspan above the surface.
   B—twice the length of the wingspan above the surface.
   C—a higher-than-normal angle of attack.

4. (Refer to Figure 2-1.) An aircraft departs an airport in the eastern daylight time zone at 0945 EDT for a 2-hour flight to an airport located in the central daylight time zone. The landing should be at what coordinated universal time?

   A—1345Z.
   B—1445Z.
   C—1545Z.

5. (Refer to Figure 2-1.) An aircraft departs an airport in the mountain standard time zone at 1615 MST for a 2-hour 15-minute flight to an airport located in the Pacific standard time zone. The estimated time of arrival at the destination airport should be

   A—1630 PST.
   B—1730 PST.
   C—1830 PST.

6. (Refer to Map 1, area 4, on Page 99.) The CTAF/UNICOM frequency at Jamestown Airport is

   A—122.0 MHz.
   B—123.0 MHz.
   C—123.6 MHz.

7. How should contact be established with an En Route Flight Advisory Service (EFAS) station, and what service would be expected?

   A—Call EFAS on 122.2 for routine weather, current reports on hazardous weather, and altimeter settings.
   B—Call flight assistance on 122.5 for advisory service pertaining to severe weather.
   C—Call Flight Watch on 122.0 for information regarding actual weather and thunderstorm activity along proposed route.

8. (Refer to Map 2, area 2, on Page 100; and Figure 2-2.) At Coeur D'Alene which frequency should be used as a Common Traffic Advisory Frequency (CTAF) to monitor airport traffic?

   A—119.1 MHz.
   B—122.1/108.8 MHz.
   C—122.8 MHz.

9. (Refer to Map 2, area 2, on Page 100; and Figure 2-2.) What is the correct UNICOM frequency to be used at Coeur D'Alene to request fuel?

   A—119.1 MHz.
   B—122.1/108.8 MHz.
   C—122.8 MHz.

10. (Refer to Map 2, on Page 100; area 2; and Figure 2-2.) At Coeur D'Alene, which frequency should be used as a Common Traffic Advisory Frequency (CTAF) to self-announce position and intentions?

    A—122.05 MHz.
    B—122.1/108.8 MHz.
    C—122.8 MHz.

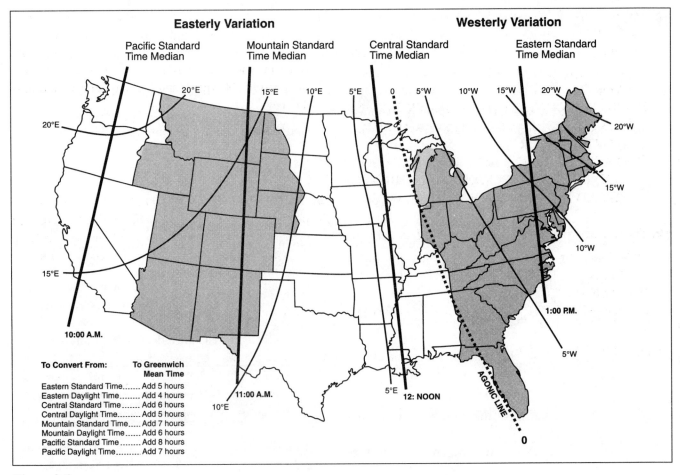

Figure 2-1

```
- - - - - - - - - - - - - - - - - - - - - - - - - - - - - - - - - - - - - - - - - - - - -
  COEUR D'ALENE AIR TERMINAL   (COE)  9 NW   UTC-8(-7DT)   N47°46.46' W116°49.17'       GREAT FALLS
    2318   B   S4   FUEL 80, 100, JET A   OX 1, 2                                       H-1B, L-9A
    RWY 05-23: H7400X140 (ASPH-GRVD)   S-57, D-95, DT-165   HIRL   0.7%up NE                 IAP
      RWY 05: MALSR.        RWY 23: REIL. VASI(V4L)—GA 3.0° TCH 39'.
    RWY 01-19: H5400X75 (ASPH)   S-50, D-83, DT-150   MIRL
      RWY 01: REIL. Rgt tfc.
    AIRPORT REMARKS: Attended Mon-Fri 1500-0100Z‡. Rwy 05-23 potential standing water and/or ice on center 3000'
      of rwy. Arpt conditions avbl on UNICOM. Rwy 19 is designated calm wind rwy. ACTIVATE MIRL Rwy 01-19, HIRL
      Rwy 05-23 and MALSR Rwy 05—CTAF. REIL Rwy 23 opr only when HIRL on high ints.
    WEATHER DATA SOURCES: AWOS-3 135.075 (208) 772-8215.
    COMMUNICATIONS: CTAF/UNICOM 122.8
      BOISE FSS (BOI) TF 1-800-WX-BRIEF. NOTAM FILE COE.
      RCO 122.05 (BOISE FSS)
    Ⓡ SPOKANE APP/DEP CON 132.1
    RADIO AIDS TO NAVIGATION: NOTAM FILE COE.
      (T) VORW/DME 108.8   COE   Chan 25   N47°46.42' W116°49.24'   at fld. 2290/19E.
        DME portion unusable 280°-350° byd 15 NM blo 11000' 220°-240° byd 15 NM.
      LEENY NDB (LOM) 347   CO   N47°44.57' W116°57.66'   053° 6.0 NM to fld.
      ILS 110.7   I-COE   Rwy 05   LOM LEENY NDB. ILS localizer/glide slope unmonitored.
- - - - - - - - - - - - - - - - - - - - - - - - - - - - - - - - - - - - - - - - - - - - - -
```

Figure 2-2

11. When flying HAWK N666CB, the proper phraseology for initial contact with McAlester AFSS is

A—"MC ALESTER RADIO, HAWK SIX SIX SIX CHARLIE BRAVO, RECEIVING ARDMORE VORTAC, OVER."
B—"MC ALESTER STATION, HAWK SIX SIX SIX CEE BEE, RECEIVING ARDMORE VORTAC, OVER."
C—"MC ALESTER FLIGHT SERVICE STATION, HAWK NOVEMBER SIX CHARLIE BRAVO, RECEIVING ARDMORE VORTAC, OVER."

12. The correct method of stating 10,500 feet MSL to ATC is

A—"TEN THOUSAND, FIVE HUNDRED FEET."
B—"TEN POINT FIVE."
C—"ONE ZERO THOUSAND, FIVE HUNDRED."

13. (Refer to Map 2, area 3, on Page 100.) Determine the approximate latitude and longitude of Shoshone County Airport.

A—47°02'N- 116°11'W.
B—47°32'N- 116°11'W.
C—47°32'N- 116°41'W.

14. (Refer to Map 3, area 2, on Page 101.) The elevation of the Chesapeake Municipal Airport is

A—20 feet.
B—36 feet.
C—360 feet.

15. (Refer to Map 4 on Page 102.) Which public use airports depicted are indicated as having fuel?

A—Minot and Mercer County Regional Airport.
B—Minot and Garrison.
C—Mercer County Regional Airport and Garrison.

16. (Refer to Map 1 on Page 99.) Determine the magnetic course from Breckheimer (Pvt) Airport (area 1) to Jamestown Airport (area 4).

A—013°.
B—021°.
C—181°.

17. (Refer to Map 4 on Page 102.) Determine the magnetic heading for a flight from Mercer County Regional Airport (area 3) to Minot International (area 1). The wind is from 330° at 25 knots, the true airspeed is 100 knots, and the magnetic variation is 11° east.

A—002°.
B—012°.
C—352°.

18. (Refer to Map 2 on Page 100.) What is the estimated time en route for a flight from St. Maries Airport (area 4) to Priest River Airport (area 1)? The wind is from 300° at 14 knots and the true airspeed is 90 knots. Add 3 minutes for climb-out.

A—38 minutes.
B—43 minutes.
C—48 minutes.

19. (Refer to Map 3 on Page 101.) What is your approximate position on low altitude airway Victor 1, southwest of Norfolk (area 1), if the VOR receiver indicates you are on the 340° radial of Elizabeth City VOR (area 3)?

A—15 nautical miles from Norfolk VORTAC.
B—18 nautical miles from Norfolk VORTAC.
C—23 nautical miles from Norfolk VORTAC.

20. (Refer to Map 5 on Page 103.) While en route on Victor 185, a flight crosses the 248° radial of Allendale VOR at 0951 and then crosses the 216 radial of Allendale VOR at 1000. What is the estimated time of arrival at Savannah VORTAC?

A—1023.
B—1028.
C—1036.

21. (Refer to Figure 2-3.) What is the relative bearing TO the station?

    A—190°.
    B—235°.
    C—315°.

22. (Refer to Figure 2-4.) If the magnetic bearing TO the station is 030°, the magnetic heading is

    A—060°.
    B—120°.
    C—270°.

23. (Refer to Map 6 on Page 104.) Estimate the time en route from Addison (area 2) to Redbird (area 3). The wind is from 300° at 15 knots, the true airspeed is 120 knots, and the magnetic variation is 7° east.

    A—8 minutes.
    B—11 minutes.
    C—14 minutes.

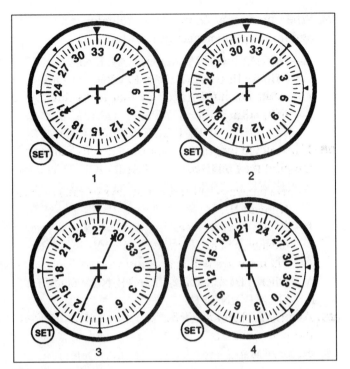

Figure 2-3

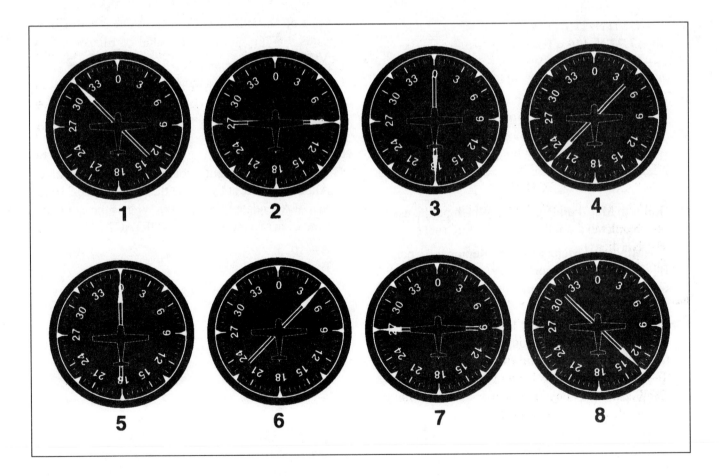

Figure 2-4

24. After landing at a tower-controlled airport, when should the pilot contact ground control?

A—When advised by the tower to do so.
B—Prior to turning off the runway.
C—After reaching a taxiway that leads directly to the parking area.

25. If instructed by ground control to taxi to Runway 9, the pilot may proceed

A—via taxiways and across runways to, but not onto, Runway 9.
B—to the next intersecting runway where further clearance is required.
C—via taxiways and across runways to Runway 9, where an immediate takeoff may be made.

26. Automatic Terminal Information Service (ATIS) is the continuous broadcast of recorded information concerning

A—pilots of radar-identified aircraft whose aircraft is in dangerous proximity to terrain or to an obstruction.
B—nonessential information to reduce frequency congestion.
C—noncontrol information in selected high-activity terminal areas.

27. An ATC radar facility issues the following advisory to a pilot flying on a heading of 360°:
"TRAFFIC 10 O'CLOCK,
2 MILES, SOUTHBOUND..."
Where should the pilot look for this traffic?

A—Northwest.
B—Northeast.
C—Southwest.

28. If the aircraft's radio fails, what is the recommended procedure when landing at a controlled airport?

A—Observe the traffic flow, enter the pattern, and look for a light signal from the tower.
B—Enter a crosswind leg and rock the wings.
C—Flash the landing lights and cycle the landing gear while circling the airport.

29. When activated, an ELT transmits on

A—123.0 and 119.0 MHz.
B—121.5 and 243.0 MHz.
C—118.0 and 118.8 MHz.

30. When making routine transponder code changes, pilots should avoid inadvertant selection of which codes?

A—3100, 7600, 7700.
B—7500, 7600, 7700.
C—7000, 7600, 7700.

31. To use VHF/DF facilities for assistance in locating an aircraft's position, the aircraft must have

A—a VHF transmitter and receiver.
B—an IFF transponder.
C—a VOR receiver and DME.

32. Frost on the wings of an airplane may

A—cause the airplane to become airborne with a lower angle of attack and at a lower indicated airspeed.
B—make it difficult or impossible to become airborne.
C—present no problems since frost will blow off when the airplane starts moving during takeoff.

33. How should the controls be held while taxiing a tri- cycle-gear equipped airplane into a left quartering headwind as depicted by A in Figure 2-5?

A—Left aileron up, neutral elevator.
B—Left aileron down, neutral elevator.
C—Left aileron up, down elevator.

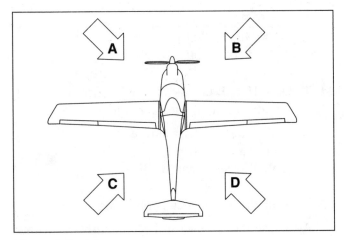

Figure 2-5

34. On the what frequency can a pilot receive a Tran- scribed Weather Broadcast in the area depicted by Map 4 on Page 102?

A—117.1 MHz.
B—118.0 MHz.
C—122.0 MHz.

35. Wing-tip vortices, the dangerous turbulence that might be encountered behind a large aircraft, are cre- ated only when that aircraft is

A—heavily loaded.
B—developing lift.
C—using high power settings.

36. When landing behind a large aircraft, the pilot should avoid wake turbulence by staying

A—above the large aircraft's final approach path and landing beyond the large aircraft's touchdown point.
B—below the large aircraft's final approach path and landing before the large aircraft's touchdown point.
C—above the large aircraft's final approach path and landing before the large aircraft's touchdown point.

37. (Refer to Figure 2-6.) The segmented circle indicates that the airport traffic is

A—left-hand for Runway 35 and right-hand for Runway 17.
B—left-hand for Runway 17 and right-hand for Runway 35.
C—right-hand for Runway 9 and left-hand for Runway 27.

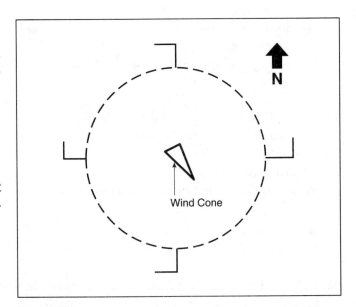

Figure 2-6

38. An airport's rotating beacon operated during daylight hours indicates

A—there are obstructions on the airport.
B—that weather at the airport located in Class D airspace is below basic VFR weather minimums.
C—the Air Traffic Control tower is not in operation.

39. When approaching to land on a runway served by a visual approach slope indicator (VASI), the pilot shall

A—maintain an altitude that captures the glide slope at least 2 miles downwind from the runway threshold.
B—maintain an altitude at or above the glide slope.
C—remain on the glide slope and land between the two-light bar.

40. (Refer to Figure 2-7.) That portion of the runway identified by the letter A may be used for

A—landing.
B—taxiing and takeoff.
C—taxiing and landing.

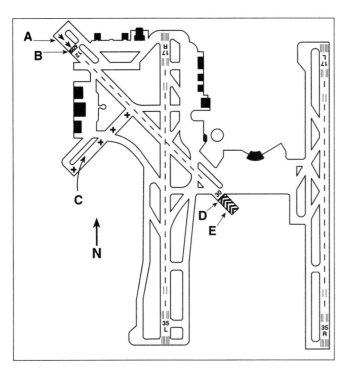

Figure 2-7

41. (Refer to Figure 2-8.) If the wind is as shown by the landing direction indicator, the pilot should land on

A—Runway 18 and expect a crosswind from the right.
B—Runway 22 directly into the wind.
C—Runway 36 and expect a crosswind from the right.

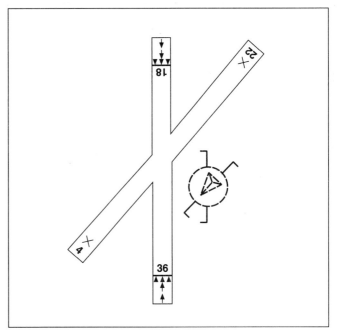

Figure 2-8

42. The numbers 9 and 27 on a runway indicate that the runway is oriented approximately

A—009° and 027° true.
B—090° and 270° true.
C—090° and 270° magnetic.

43. If instructed by ground control to taxi to Runway 9, the pilot may proceed

A—via taxiways and across runways to, but not onto, Runway 9.
B—to the next intersecting runway where further clearance is required.
C—via taxiways and across runways to Runway 9, where an immediate takeoff may be made.

44. While on final approach for landing, an alternating green and red light followed by a flashing red light is received from the control tower. Under these circumstances, the pilot should

   A—discontinue the approach, fly the same traffic pattern and approach again, and land.
   B—exercise extreme caution and abandon the approach, realizing the airport is unsafe for landing.
   C—abandon the approach, circle the airport to the right, and expect a flashing white light when the airport is safe for landing.

45. Which is the correct traffic pattern departure procedure to use at a noncontrolled airport?

   A—Depart in any direction consistent with safety, after crossing the airport boundary.
   B—Make all turns to the left.
   C—Comply with any FAA traffic pattern established to the airport.

46. Ceiling, as used in weather reports, is defined as the height above the Earth's surface of the

   A—lowest reported obscuration and the highest layer of clouds reported as overcast.
   B—lowest layer of clouds reported as broken or overcast and not classified as thin.
   C—lowest layer of clouds reported as scattered, broken, or thin.

47. A temperature inversion would most likely result in which weather condition?

   A—Good visibility in the lower levels of the atmosphere and poor visibility above an inversion aloft.
   B—An increase in temperature as altitude is increased.
   C—A decrease in temperature as altitude is increased.

48. What are the standard temperature and pressure values for sea level?

   A—15°C and 29.92" Hg.
   B—59°C and 1013.2 millibars.
   C—59°C and 29.92 millibars.

49. What is meant by the term dew point?

   A—The temperature at which condensation and evaporation are equal.
   B—The temperature at which dew will always form.
   C—The temperature to which air must be cooled to become saturated.

50. Clouds, fog, and dew will always form when

   A—water vapor condenses.
   B—relative humidity reaches or exceeds 100 percent.
   C—the temperature and dew point are equal.

51. Which of the following would decrease the stability of an air mass?

   A—Warming from below.
   B—Cooling from below.
   C—Decrease in water vapor.

52. If an unstable air mass is forced upward, what type of clouds can be expected?

   A—Layer-like clouds with little vertical development.
   B—Layer-like clouds with considerable associated turbulence.
   C—Clouds with considerable vertical development and associated turbulence.

53. An almond or lens-shaped cloud which appears stationary, but which may contain wind of 50 kts. or more, is referred to as

   A—an inactive frontal cloud.
   B—a funnel cloud.
   C—a lenticular cloud.

54. Which clouds have the greatest turbulence?

   A—Towering cumulus.
   B—Cumulonimbus.
   C—Nimbostratus.

55. What are characteristics of unstable air?

   A—Turbulence and good surface visibility.
   B—Turbulence and poor surface visibility.
   C—Nimbostratus clouds and good surface visibility.

56. Hazardous wind shear is commonly encountered near the ground

    A—near thunderstorms and during periods when the wind velocity is stronger than 35 knots.
    B—during periods when the wind velocity is stronger than 35 knots and near mountain valleys.
    C—during periods of strong temperature inversion and near thunderstorms.

57. One in-flight condition necessary for structural icing to form is

    A—small temperature/dew point spread.
    B—stratiform clouds.
    C—visible moisture.

58. Thunderstorms which generally produce the most intense hazard to aircraft are

    A—steady-state thunderstorms.
    B—warm front thunderstorms.
    C—squall line thunderstorms.

59. If there is thunderstorm activity in the vicinity of an airport at which you plan to land, which hazardous and invisible atmospheric phenomenon might be expected on the landing approach?

    A—St. Elmo's fire.
    B—Wind shear turbulence.
    C—Virga.

60. Upon encountering severe turbulence, which condition should the pilot attempt to maintain?

    A—Constant altitude.
    B—Constant airspeed (V_A).
    C—Level flight altitude.

61. In which situation is advection fog most likely to form?

    A—A warm, moist air mass on the windward side of mountains.
    B—An air mass moving inland from the coast in winter.
    C—A light breeze blowing colder air out to sea.

62. To best detemine forecast weather conditions between weather reporting stations, the pilot should refer to

    A—pilot reports.
    B—weather maps.
    C—Area forecasts.

63. To get a complete weather briefing for the planned flight, the pilot should request

    A—an outlook briefing.
    B—a general briefing.
    C—a standard briefing.

64. SIGMETs are issued as a warning of weather conditions hazardous

    A—to all aircraft.
    B—only to light aircraft operations.
    C—particularly to heavy aircraft.

65. What information is provided by the Radar Summary Chart that is not shown on other weather charts?

    A—Lines and cells of hazardous thunderstorms.
    B—Ceilings and precipitation between reporting stations.
    C—Types of precipitation between reporting stations.

```
FD WBC 151745
BASED ON 151200Z DATA
VALID 1600Z FOR USE 1800-0300Z.  TEMPS NEG ABV 24000


FT      3000    6000     9000      12000     18000     24000     30000    34000    39000
ALS                      2420      2635-08   2535-18   2444-30   245945   246755   246862
AMA             2714     2725+00   2625-04   2531-15   2542-27   265842   256352   256762
DEN                      2321-04   2532-08   2434-19   2441-31   235347   236056   236262
HLC             1707-01  2113-03   2219-07   2330-17   2435-30   244145   244854   245561
MKC     0507    2006+03  2215-01   2322-06   2338-17   2348-29   236143   237252   238160
STL     2113    2325+07  2332+02   2339-04   2356-16   2373-27   239440   730649   731960
```

Figure 2-9

66. (Refer to Figure 2-9.) What wind is forecast for STL at 18,000 feet?

A—230° true at 56 knots.

B—235° true at 06 knots.

C—235° magnetic at 06, peak gusts to 16 knots.

67. (Refer to Figure 2-10.) Of what value is the Weather Depiction Chart to the pilot?

A—For determining general weather conditions on which to base flight planning.

B—For a forecast of cloud coverage, visibilities, and frontal activity.

C—For determining frontal trends and air mass characteristics.

68. (Refer to Figure 2-11.) What weather is forecast for the Gulf Coast area just ahead of the cold front during the first 12 hours?

A—Ceiling 1,000 to 3,000 feet and/or visibility 3 to 5 miles with intermittent thundershowers and rain showers.

B—IFR with moderate or greater turbulence over the coastal areas.

C—Rain and thunderstorms moving northeastward ahead of the front.

69. (Refer to Figure 2-12, area B.) What does the dashed line enclose?

A—Areas of heavy rain.

B—Severe weather watch area.

C—Areas of hail 1/4 inch in diameter.

70. (Refer to Figure 2-12, area D.) The top of the precipitation is

A—2,000 feet.

B—20,000 feet.

C—30,000 feet.

71. (Refer to Figure 2-13.) Which of the reporting stations have VFR weather?

A—All.

B—KINK, KBOI, and KJFK.

C—KINK, KBOI, and KLAX.

72. (Refer to Figure 2-13.) What are the current conditions depicted for Chicago Midway Airport (KMDW)?

A—Sky 700 feet overcast, visibility 1-1/2 SM, rain

B—Sky 7000 feet overcast, visibility 1-1/2 SM, heavy rain

C—Sky 700 feet overcast, visibility 11, occasionally 2 SM, with rain.

73. (Refer to Figure 2-14.) The base and tops of the overcast layer reported by a pilot are

A—1,800 feet MSL and 5,500 feet MSL.

B—5,500 feet AGL and 7,200 feet MSL.

C—7,200 feet MSL and 8,900 feet MSL.

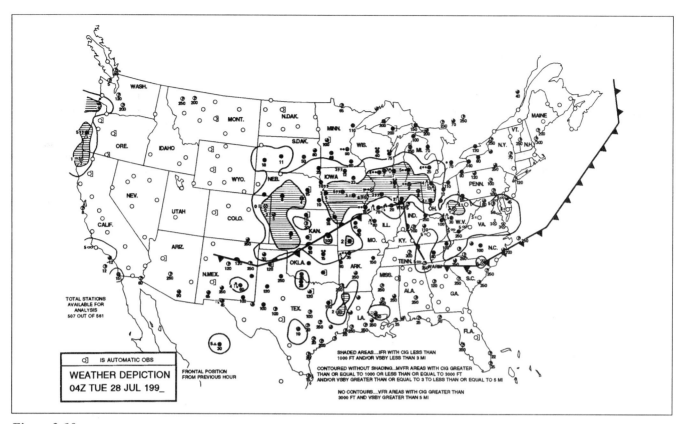

Figure 2-10

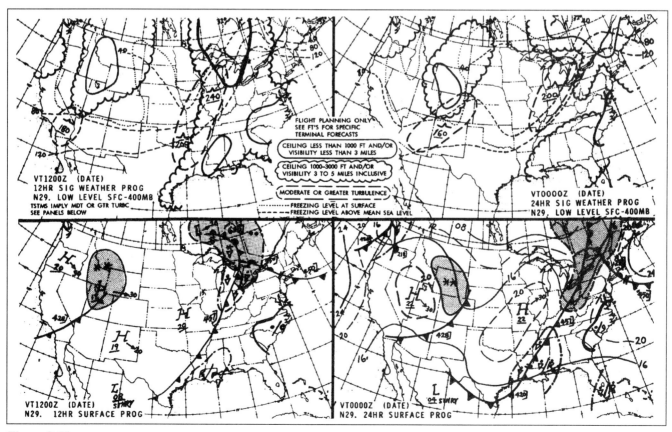

Figure 2-11

74. (Refer to Figure 2-15.) During the time period from 0600Z to 0800Z, what significant weather is forecast for KOKC?

A—Wind – 210° at 15 knots.

B—Visibility – possibly 6 statute miles with scattered clouds at 4,000 feet.

C—No significant weather is forecast for this time period.

75. (Refer to Figure 2-16.) What sky condition and type obstructions to vision are forecast for all the area except TN from 1040Z until 2300Z?

A—Ceilings 3,000 to 5,000 feet broken, visibility 3 to 5 miles in fog.

B—8,000 feet scattered to clear except visibility below 3 miles in fog until 1500Z over south-central Texas.

C—Generally ceilings 3,000 to 8,000 feet to clear with visibility sometimes below 3 miles in fog.

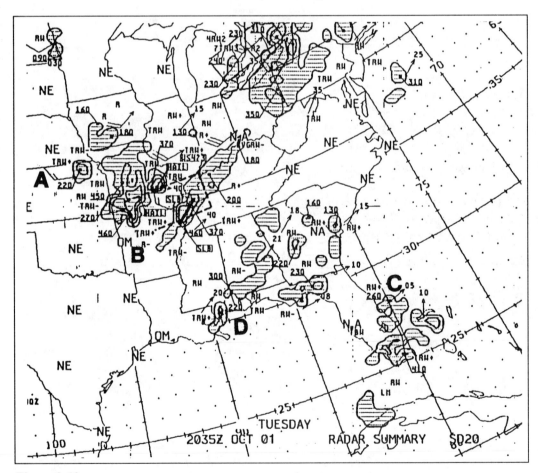

Figure 2-12

```
METAR KINK 121845Z 11012G18KT 15SM SKC 25/17 A3000

METAR KBOI 121854Z 13004KT 30SM SCT150 17/6 A3015

METAR KLAX 121852Z 25004KT 6SM BR SCT007 SCT250 16/15 A2991

SPECI KMDW 121856Z 32005KT 1 1/2SM RA OVC007 17/16 A2980 RMK
RAB35

SPECI KJFK 121853Z 18004KT 1/2SM FG R04/2200 OVC005 20/18 A3006
```

Figure 2-13

```
UA /OV OKC–TUL /TM 1800 /FL 120 /TP BE90 /SK 018 BKN 055 /
/072 OVC 089 /CLR ABV /TA –9/WV 0921/TB MDT 055–072 /IC LGT–MDT
CLR 072–089.
```

Figure 2-14

```
TAF

KMEM   121720Z 121818 20012KT 5SM HZ BKN030 PROB40 2022 1SM TSRA OVC008CB
       FM2200 33015G20KT P6SM BKN015 OVC025 PROB40 2202 3SM SHRA
       FM0200 35012KT OVC008 PROB40 0205 2SM -RASN BECMG 0608 02008KT NSW BKN012
        BECMG 1012 00000KT 3SM BR SKC TEMPO 1214 1/2SM FG
       FM1600 VRB04KT P6SM NSW SKC=

KOKC   051130Z 051212 14008KT 5SM BR BKN030 TEMPO 1316 1 1/2SM BR
       FM1600 16010KT P6SM NSW SKC BECMG 2224 20013G20KT 4SM SHRA OVC020
        PROB40 0006 2SM TSRA OVC008CB BECMG 0608 21015KT P6SM NSW SCT040=
```

Figure 2-15

```
DFWH FA Ø41Ø4Ø
HAZARDS VALID UNTIL Ø423ØØ
OK TX AR LA TN MS AL AND CSTL WTRS
FLT PRCTNS. . .TURBC. . .TN AL AND CSTL WTRS
               . . .ICG. . .TN
               . . .IFR. . .TX
TSTMS IMPLY PSBL SVR OR GTR TURBC SVR ICG AND LLWS
NON MSL HGTS NOTED BY AGL OR CIG
THIS FA ISSUANCE INCORPORATES THE FOLLOWING AIRMETS STILL IN
EFFECT. . .NONE.


DFWS FA Ø41Ø4Ø
SYNOPSIS VALID UNTIL Ø5Ø5ØØ
AT 11Z RDG OF HI PRES ERN TX NWWD TO CNTRL CO WITH HI CNTR
OVR ERN TX.  BY Ø5Z HI CNTR MOVS TO CNTRL LA.


DFWI FA Ø41Ø4Ø
ICING AND FRZLVL VALID UNTIL Ø423ØØ
TN
FROM SLK TO HAT TO MEM TO ORD TO SLK
OCNL MDT RIME ICGIC ABV FRZLVL TO 1ØØ. CONDS ENDING BY 17Z.
FRZLVL 8Ø CHA SGF LINE SLPG TO 12Ø S OF A IAH MAF LINE.


DFWT FA Ø41Ø4Ø
TURBC VALID UNTIL Ø423ØØ
TN AL AND CSTL WTRS
FROM SLK TO FLO TO 9ØS MOB TO MEI TO BUF TO SLK
OCNL MDT TURBC 25Ø-38Ø DUE TO JTSTR. CONDS MOVG SLOLY EWD
AND CONTG BYD 23Z.


DFWC FA O41Ø4Ø
SGFNT CLOUD AND WX VALID UNTIL Ø423ØØ. . . OTLK Ø423ØØ-Ø5Ø5ØØ
IFR. . .TX
FROM SAT TO PSX TO BRO TO MOB TO SAT
VSBY BLO 3F TIL 15Z.
OK AR TX LA MS AL AND CSTL WTRS
8Ø SCT TO CLR EXCP VSBY BLO 3F TIL 15Z OVR PTNS S CNTRL TX.
OTLK. . .VFR.
TN
CIGS 3Ø-5Ø BKN IØØ VSBYS OCNLY 3-5F BCMG AGL 4Ø-5Ø SCT TO
CLR BY 19Z. OTLK. . .VFR.
```

Figure 2-16

Stage 3 Exam

1. What type of oxygen should be used to replenish an aircraft's oxygen for high altitude flights?

   A—Medical oxygen.
   B—Welder's oxygen.
   C—Aviation breathing oxygen.

2. (Refer to Map 1 on Page 99.) What hazards to aircraft may exist in areas such as Devils Lake East MOA?

   A—Unusual, often invisible, hazards to aircraft such as artillery firing.
   B—High density military training activities.
   C—Parachute jump operations.

3. (Refer to Map 1, area 6, on Page 99.) The airspace overlying and within 5 miles of Barnes County Airport is

   A—Class D airspace from the surface to the floor of the overlying Class E airspace.
   B—Class E airspace from the surface to 1,200 feet MSL.
   C—Class G airspace from the surface to 700 feet AGL.

4. (Refer to Map 1, area 2, on Page 99.) The visibility and cloud clearance requirements to operate VFR during daylight hours over Cooperstown Airport between 1,200 feet AGL and 10,000 feet MSL are

   A—1 mile and clear of clouds.
   B—1 mile and 1,000 feet above, 500 feet below, and 2,000 feet horizontally from clouds.
   C—3 miles and 1,000 feet above, 500 feet below, and 2,000 feet horizontally from clouds.

5. (Refer to Map 3, area 1, on Page 101.) What minimum radio equipment is required to land and take off at Norfolk International?

   A—Mode C transponder and omnireceiver.
   B—Mode C transponder and two-way radio.
   C—Mode C transponder, omnireceiver, and DME.

6. (Refer to Map 2, area 3, on Page 100.) The vertical limits of that portion of Class E airspace designated as a Federal Airway over Magee Airport are

   A—1,200 feet AGL to 10,000 feet MSL.
   B—7,500 feet MSL to l2,500 feet MSL.
   C—7,500 feet MSL to 17,999 feet MSL.

7. What minimum radio equipment is required for VFR operation within Class B airspace?

   A—Two-way radio communications equipment and a 4096-code transponder.
   B—Two-way radio communications equipment, a 4096-code transponder, and an encoding altimeter.
   C—Two-way radio communications equipment, a 4096-code transponder, an encoding altimeter, and a VOR or TACAN receiver.

8. (Refer to Map 5, area 3, on Page 103.) What is the floor of the Savannah Class C airspace at the outer circle?

   A—1,200 feet AGL.
   B—1,300 feet MSL.
   C—1,700 feet MSL.

9. (Refer to Map 3, area 2, on Page 101.) The flag symbol at Lake Drummond represents a

   A—compulsory reporting point for Norfolk Class C airspace.
   B—compulsory reporting point for Hampton Roads Airport.
   C—visual checkpoint used to identify position for initial callup to Norfolk Approach Control.

10. What special check should be made on an aircraft during preflight after it has been stored an extended period of time?

    A—ELT batteries and operation.
    B—Condensation in the fuel tanks.
    C—Damage or obstruction caused by animals, birds, or insects.

11. Under what condition, if any, may civil pilots enter a restricted area?

A—With the controlling agency's authorization.
B—On airways with ATC clearance.
C—Under no condition.

12. All operations within Class C airspace must be in

A—accordance with instrument flight rules.
B—compliance with ATC clearances and instructions.
C—an aircraft equipped with a 4096-code transponder with Mode C encoding capability.

13. How should a VFR flight plan be closed at the completion of the flight at a controlled airport?

A—The tower will automatically close the flight plan when the aircraft turns off the runway.
B—The pilot must close the flight plan with the nearest FSS of other FAA facility upon landing.
C—The tower will relay the instructions to the nearest FSS when the aircraft contacts the tower for landing.

14. (Refer to Map 7, area 1, on Page 105.) What minimum altitude is necessary to vertically clear the obstacle on the northeast side of Airpark East Airport by 500 feet?

A—1,010 feet MSL.
B—1,273 feet MSL.
C—1,283 feet MSL.

15. (Refer to Figure 3-1.) What is the recommended communications procedure for landing at Lincoln Municipal during the hours when the tower is not in operation?

A—Monitor airport traffic and announce your position and intentions on 118.5 MHz.
B—Contact UNICOM on 122.95 MHz for traffic advisories.
C—Monitor ATIS for airport conditions, then announce your position on 122.95 MHz.

16. The most effective method of scanning for other aircraft for collision avoidance during nighttime hours is to use

A—regularly spaced concentration on the 3-, 9-, and 12-o'clock positions.
B—a series of short, regularly spaced eye movements to search each 30-degree sector.
C—peripheral vision by scanning small sectors and utilizing offcenter viewing.

17. How can you determine if another aircraft is on a collision course with your aircraft?

A—The other aircraft will always appear to get larger and closer at a rapid rate.
B—The nose of each aircraft is pointed at the same point in space.
C—There will be no apparent relative motion between your aircraft and the other aircraft.

18. Prior to starting each maneuver, pilots should

A—check altitude, airspeed, and heading indications.
B—visually scan the entire area for collision avoidance.
C—announce their intentions on the nearest CTAF.

19. How long does the Airworthiness Certificate of an aircraft remain valid?

A—As long as the aircraft has a current Registration Certificate.
B—Indefinitely, unless the aircraft suffers major damage.
C—As long as the aircraft is maintained and operated as required by Federal Aviation Regulations.

20. FAA advisory circulars (some free, others at cost) are available to all pilots and are obtained by

A—distribution from the nearest FAA district office.
B—ordering those desired from the Government Printing Office.
C—subscribing to the Federal Register.

21. To preclude the effects of hypoxia,

A—avoid flying above 10,000 ft. MSL for prolonged periods without breathing supplemental oxygen.
B—rely on your body's built-in alarm system to warn when you are not getting enough oxygen.
C—try swallowing, yawning, or holding the nose and mouth shut and forcibly try to exhale.

LINCOLN MUNI   (LNK)   4 NW   UTC–6(–5DT)   N40°51.05' W96°45.55'   **OMAHA**
     1218   B   S4   **FUEL** 100LL, JET A   TPA—2218(1000)   ARFF Index B   H–1E, 3F, 4F, L–11B
     RWY 17R–35L: H12901X200 (ASPH–CONC–GRVD)   S–100, D–200, DT–400   HIRL   IAP
       RWY 17R: MALSR. VASI(V4L)—GA 3.0° TCH 55'. Rgt tfc.   0.4% down.
       RWY 35L: MALSR. VASI(V4L)—GA 3.0° TCH 55'.
     RWY 14–32: H8620X150 (ASPH–CONC–GRVD)   S–80, D–170, DT–280   MIRL
       RWY 14: REIL. VASI(V4L)—GA 3.0° TCH 48'.
       RWY 32: VASI(V4L)—GA 3.0° TCH 53'. Thld dsplcd 431'. Pole.   0.3% up.
     RWY 17L–35R: H5400X100 (ASPH–CONC–AFSC)   S–49, D–60   HIRL   0.8% up N
       RWY 17L: PAPI(P4L)—GA 3.0° TCH 33'.   RWY 35R: PAPI(P4L)—GA 3.0° TCH 40'. Pole. Rgt tfc.
     AIRPORT REMARKS: Attended continuously. Birds in vicinity of arpt. Twy D clsd between taxiways S and H indef. For
       MALSR Rwy 17R and Rwy 35L ctc twr. When twr clsd MALSR Rwy 17R and Rwy 35L preset on med ints, and REIL
       Rwy 14 left on when wind favor. NOTE: See Land and Hold Short Operations Section.
     WEATHER DATA SOURCES: ASOS (402) 474–9214. LLWAS
     COMMUNICATIONS: CTAF 118.5   ATIS 118.05   UNICOM 122.95
       COLUMBUS FSS (OLU) TF 1–800–WX–BRIEF. NOTAM FILE LNK.
       RCO 122.65 (COLUMBUS FSS)
    ®️ **APP/DEP CON** 124.0 (170°–349°) 124.8 (350°–169°) (1130–0630Z‡)
    ®️ **MINNEAPOLIS CENTER APP/DEP CON** 128.75 (0630–1130Z‡)
       TOWER 118.5 125.7 (1130–0630Z‡)   **GND CON** 121.9   **CLNC DEL** 120.7
     AIRSPACE: CLASS C svc 1130–0630Z‡ ctc **APP CON** other times **CLASS E.**
     RADIO AIDS TO NAVIGATION: NOTAM FILE LNK. VHF/DF ctc FSS.
       (H) VORTACW 116.1   LNK   Chan 108   N40°55.43' W96°44.52'   181° 4.5 NM to fld. 1370/9E
       POTTS NDB (MHW/LOM) 385   LN   N40°44.83' W96°45.75'   355° 6.2 NM to fld. Unmonitored when twr clsd.
       ILS 111.1   I–OCZ   Rwy 17R.   MM and OM unmonitored.
       ILS 109.9   I–LNK   Rwy 35L   LOM POTTS NDB. MM unmonitored. LOM unmonitored when twr clsd.
     COMM/NAVAID REMARKS: Emerg frequency 121.5 not available at tower.

LOUP CITY MUNI   (NE03)   1 NW   UTC–6(–5DT)   N41°17.42' W98°59.44'   **OMAHA**
     2070   B   **FUEL** 100LL   L–11B
     RWY 15–33: H3200X50 (ASPH)   S–8   LIRL
       RWY 33: Trees.
     RWY 04–22: 2100X100 (TURF)
       RWY 04: Tree.   RWY 22: Road.
     AIRPORT REMARKS: Unattended. For svc call 308–745–0328/1244/0664.
     COMMUNICATIONS: CTAF 122.9
       COLUMBUS FSS (OLU) TF 1–800–WX–BRIEF. NOTAM FILE OLU.
     RADIO AIDS TO NAVIGATION: NOTAM FILE OLU.
       WOLBACH (H) VORTAC 114.8   OBH   Chan 95   N41°22.54' W98°21.22'   253° 29.3 NM to fld. 2010/7E.

MARTIN FLD   (See SO SIOUX CITY)

MC COOK MUNI   (MCK)   2 E   UTC–6(–5DT)   N40°12.36' W100°35.51'   **OMAHA**
     2579   B   S4   **FUEL** 100LL, JET A   ARFF Index Ltd.   H–2D, L–11A
     RWY 12–30: H5999X100 (CONC)   S–30, D–38   MIRL   0.6% up NW   IAP
       RWY 12: MALS. VASI(V4L)—GA 3.0° TCH 33'. Tree.   RWY 30: REIL. VASI(V4L)—GA 3.0° TCH 42'.
     RWY 03–21: H3999X75 (CONC)   S–30, D–38   MIRL
       RWY 03: VASI(V2L)—GA 3.0° TCH 26'. Rgt tfc.   RWY 21: VASI(V2L)—GA 3.0° TCH 26'.
     RWY 17–35: 1350X200 (TURF)
     AIRPORT REMARKS: Attended daylight hours. Parachute Jumping. Deer on and in vicinity of arpt. Numerous
       waterfowl/migratory birds invof arpt. Arpt closed to air carrier operations with more than 30 passengers except
       24 hour PPR, call arpt manager 308–345–2022. Avoid McCook State (abandoned) arpt 7 miles NW on the MCK
       VOR/DME 313° radial at 8.3 DME. ACTIVATE VASI Rwys 12 and 30 and MALS Rwy 12—CTAF.
     COMMUNICATIONS: CTAF/UNICOM 122.8
       COLUMBUS FSS (OLU) TF 1–800–WX–BRIEF. NOTAM FILE MCK.
       RCO 122.6 (COLUMBUS FSS)
       DENVER CENTER APP/DEP CON 132.7
     AIRSPACE: CLASS E svc effective 1100–0500Z‡ except holidays other times **CLASS G.**
     RADIO AIDS TO NAVIGATION: NOTAM FILE MCK.
       (H) VORW/DME 115.3   MCK   Chan 100   N40°12.23' W100°35.65'   at fld. 2570/8E.

Figure 3-1

22. A pilot should be able to overcome the symptoms or avoid future occurrences of hyperventilation by

   A—closely monitoring the flight instruments to control the airplane.

   B—slowing the breathing rate, breathing into a bag, or talking aloud.

   C—increasing the breathing rate in order to increase lung ventilation.

23. A pilot is more subject to spatial disorientation if

   A—kinesthetic senses are ignored.

   B—eyes are moved often in the process of cross-checking the flight instruments.

   C—body signals are used to interpret flight attitude.

24. What preparation should a pilot make to adapt the eyes for night flying?

   A—Avoid red lights at least 30 minutes before the flight.

   B—Wear amber colored glasses at least 30 minutes before the flight.

   C—Avoid bright white light at least 30 minutes before the flight.

25. What effect does haze have on the ability to see traffic or terrain features during flight?

   A—Haze causes the eyes to focus on infinity.

   B—The eyes tend to overwork in haze and do not detect relative movement easily.

   C—All traffic or terrain features appear to be farther away than their actual distance.

26. Which incidents would require that an immediate notification be made to the nearest NTSB field office?

   A—An overdue aircraft that is believed to be involved in an accident.

   B—An in-flight radio (communication) failure.

   C—An in-flight generator or alternator failure.

27. Which is a class of airplane?

   A—Multi-engine land.

   B—Helicopter.

   C—Glider.

28. The definition of nighttime is

   A—sunset to sunrise.

   B—1 hour after sunset to 1 hour before sunrise.

   C—from the end of evening civil twilight to the beginning of morning civil twilight.

29. Unless otherwise specified, Federal airways extend from

   A—1,200 ft. above the surface upward to, but not including, 14,500 ft. MSL and are 16 NM wide.

   B—700 ft. above the surface upward to the Continental Control Area and are 10NM wide.

   C—1,200 ft. above the surface upward to, but not including, 18,000 ft. MSL and are 18 NM wide.

30. Private pilots acting as pilot-in-command, or in any other capacity as a required pilot flight crewmember, must have in their personal possession while aboard the aircraft

   A—a current logbook endorsement to show that a flight review has been satisfactorily accomplished.

   B—The current and appropriate pilot and medical certificates.

   C—the current endorsement on the pilot certificate to show that a flight has been satisfactorily accomplished.

31. A Third-Class Medical Certificate is issued to a 36-year-old pilot on August 10, this year. To exercise the privileges of a Private Pilot Certificate, the medical certificate will be valid until midnight on

   A—August 10, 2 years later.

   B—August 31, 3 years later.

   C—August 31, 2 years later.

32. What is the definition of a high-performance airplane?

   A—An airplane with an engine of more than 200 horsepower.

   B—An airplane with 180 horsepower, or retractable landing gear, flaps, and a fixed-pitch propeller.

   C—An airplane with a normal cruise speed in excess of 200 knots.

33. To meet the flight experience requirements to act as pilot-in-command carrying passengers at night, a pilot must have made at least three takeoffs and three landings to a full stop within the preceeding 90 days

A—in the same category and class of aircraft to be used.

B—in the same class or aircraft to be used.

C—in any aircraft, but must be accompanied by a certified flight instructor who meets the recent experience for night flight.

34. When a certificated pilot changes permanent mailing address and fails to notify the FAA Airmen Certification Branch of the new address, the pilot is entitled to exercise the privileges of the pilot certificate for a period of only

A—30 days after the date of the move.

B—60 days after the date of the move.

C—90 days after the date of the move.

35. In regard to general privileges and limitations, a private pilot may

A—not be paid in any manner for the operating expenses of a flight.

B—act as pilot-in-command of an aircraft carrying a passenger for compensation if the flight is in connection with a business or employment.

C—share the operating expenses of a flight with a passenger.

36. If an in-flight emergency requires immediate action, a pilot-in-command may

A—deviate from regulations to the extent required to meet the emergency, but must submit a written report to the Administrator within 24 hours.

B—not deviate from regulations unless prior to the deviation approval is granted by the Administrator.

C—deviate from regulations to the extent required to meet that emergency.

37. When must a pilot who deviates from a rule during an emergency send a written report of that deviation to the Administrator?

A—7 days.

B—10 days.

C—Upon request.

38. Preflight action, as required by regulations for all flights away from the vicinity of an airport, shall include a study of the weather, taking into consideration fuel requirements and

A—the designation of an alternate airport.

B—the filing of a flight plan.

C—an alternate course of action if the flight cannot be completed as planned.

39. Under what condition, if any, may a pilot allow a person who is obviously under the influence of intoxicating liquors or drugs to be carried aboard an aircraft?

A—Under no condition.

B—Only if the person is a medical patient under proper care or in an emergency.

C—Only if the person does not have access to the cockpit or pilot's compartment.

40. Regulations require that seatbelts in an airplane be properly secured about the

A—occupants during takeoffs and landings.

B—crewmembers only, during takeoffs and landings.

C—passengers and crewmembers during the entire flight.

41. What is the fuel requirement for flight under VFR at night in an airplane?

A—Enough to complete the flight at normal cruising flight with adverse wind conditions.

B—Enough to fly to the first point of intended landing and to fly after that for 30 minutes after cruising speed.

C—Enough to fly to the first point of intended landing and to fly after that for 45 minutes at normal cruising speed.

42. In addition to a valid Airworthiness Certificate, what documents or records must be aboard an aircraft during flight?

A—Radio station license and repair and alteration forms.

B—Operating limitations and Registration Certificate.

C—Radio station license and owner's manual.

43. When two or more aircraft are approaching an airport for the purpose of landing, the right-of-way belongs to the aircraft

A—that has the other to its right.

B—that is either ahead of or to the other's right regardless of altitude.

C—at the lower altitude but it shall not take advantage of this rule to cut in front of or to overtake another.

44. Except when necessary for takeoff or landing, what is the minimum safe altitude for a pilot to operate an aircraft anywhere?

A—An altitude allowing, if a power unit fails, an emergency landing without undue hazard to persons or property on the surface.

B—An altitude of 500 ft. above the surface and no closer than 500 ft. to any person, vessel, vehicle, or structure.

C—An altitude of 500 ft. above the highest obstacle with a horizontal radius of 1,000 ft.

45. Unless otherwise authorized, two-way radio communications with Air Traffic Control are required for landings or takeoffs

A—at all tower controlled airports regardless of weather conditions.

B—at all tower controlled airports only when weather conditions are less than VFR.

C—at all tower controlled airports within Class D airspace only when weather conditions are less than VFR.

46. What minimum pilot certification is required for operation within Class B airspace?

A—Recreational Pilot Certificate.

B—Private Pilot Certificate or Student Pilot Certificate with appropriate logbook endorsements.

C—Private Pilot Certificate with an instrument rating.

47. VFR flight in controlled airspace above 1,200 feet AGL and below 10,000 feet MSL requires a minimum visibility and vertical cloud clearance of

A—3 miles, and 500 feet below or 1,000 feet above the clouds in controlled airspace.

B—5 miles, and 1,000 feet below or 1,000 feet above the clouds at all altitudes.

C—5 miles, and 1,000 feet below or 1,000 feet above the clouds only in Class A airspace.

48. The basic VFR weather minimums for operating an aircraft within Class D airspace are

A—500-foot ceiling and 1 mile visibility.

B—1,000-foot ceiling and 3 miles visibility.

C—clear of clouds and 2 miles visibility.

49. What are the minimum requirements for airplane operations under special VFR in Class D airspace at night?

A—The airplane must be under radar surveillance at all times while in Class D airspace.

B—The airplane must be equipped for IFR with an altitude reporting transponder.

C—The pilot must be instrument rated, and the airplane must be IFR equipped.

50. Which VFR cruising altitude is acceptable for a flight on a Victor Airway with a magnetic course of 175°? The terrain is less than 1,000 feet.

A—4,500 feet.

B—5,000 feet.

C—5,500 feet.

Final Exam

1. What is absolute altitude?

   A—The altitude read directly from the altimeter.
   B—The vertical distance of the aircraft above the surface.
   C—The height above the standard datum plane.

2. What is density altitude?

   A—The height above the standard datum plane.
   B—The pressure altitude corrected for nonstandard temperature.
   C—The altitude read directly from the altimeter.

3. Under what condition is indicated altitude the same as true altitude?

   A—If the altimeter has no mechanical error.
   B—When at sea level under standard conditions.
   C—When at 18,000 feet MSL with the altimeter set at 29.92.

4. (Refer to Figure 1.) Determine the density altitude for these conditions:
   Altimeter setting 30.35
   Runway temperature .... +25°F
   Airport elevation .... 3,894 ft MSL

   A—2,000 feet MSL.
   B—2,900 feet MSL.
   C—3,500 feet MSL.

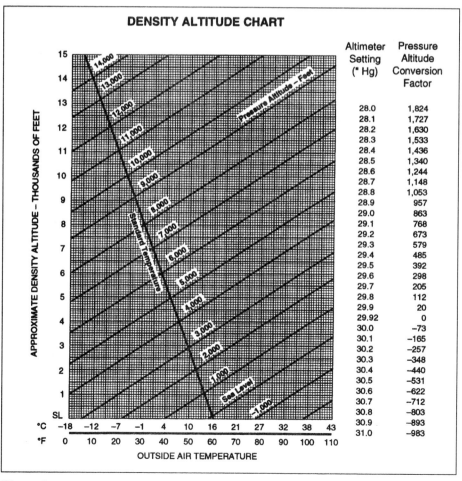

Figure 1

5. How do variations in temperature affect the altimeter?

A—Pressure levels are raised on warm days and the indicated altitude is lower than true altitude.

B—Higher temperatures expand the pressure levels and the indicated altitude is higher than true altitude.

C—Lower temperatures lower the pressure levels and the indicated altitude is lower than true altitude.

6. Applying carburetor heat will

A—result in more air going through the carburetor.

B—enrich the fuel/air mixture.

C—not affect the fuel/air mixture.

7. During the run-up at a high-elevation airport, a pilot notes a slight engine roughness that is not affected by the magneto check but grows worse during the carburetor heat check. Under these circumstances, what would be the most logical initial action?

A—Check the results obtained with a leaner setting of the mixture.

B—Taxi back to the flight line for a maintenance check.

C—Reduce manifold pressure to control detonation.

8. In the Northern Hemisphere, a magnetic compass will normally indicate initially a turn toward the west if

A—a left turn is entered from a north heading.

B—a right turn is entered from a north heading.

C—an aircraft is accelerated while on a north heading.

9. If the pitot tube and outside static vents become clogged, which instruments would be affected?

A—The altimeter, airspeed indicator, and turn-and-slip indicator.

B—The altimeter, airspeed indicator, and vertical speed indicator.

C—The altimeter, attitude indicator, and turn-and-slip indicator.

10. Which basic flight maneuver increases the load factor on an airplane as compared to straight-and-level flight?

A—Climbs.

B—Turns.

C—Stalls.

11. Floating caused by the phenomenon of ground effect will be most realized during an approach to land when at

A—less than the length of the wingspan above the surface.

B—twice the length of the wingspan above the surface.

C—a higher-than-normal angle of attack.

12. (Refer to Figure 2.) An aircraft departs an airport in the central standard time zone at 0930 CST for a 2-hour flight to an airport located in the mountain standard time zone. The landing should be at what time?

A—0930 MST.

B—1030 MST.

C—1130 MST.

13. (Refer to Map 3 on Page 101.) What is the recommended communications procedure for a landing at Currituck County Airport?

A—Transmit intentions on 122.9 MHz when 10 miles out and give position reports in the traffic pattern.

B—Contact Elizabeth City FSS for airport advisory service.

C—Contact New Bern FSS for area traffic information.

14. (Refer to Map 4, area 3, on Page 102.) Which airport is located at approximately 47°21'N latitude and 101°01'W longitude?

A—Underwood.

B—Evenson.

C—Washburn.

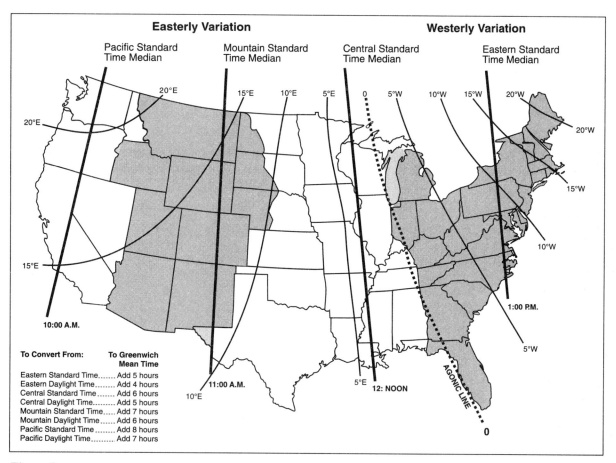

Easterly Variation

Pacific Standard Time Median

Mountain Standard Time Median

Westerly Variation

Central Standard Time Median

Eastern Standard Time Median

20°E
15°E
10°E
5°E
0
5°W
10°W
15°W
20°W
20°W

20°E

15°E

10:00 A.M.

11:00 A.M.
10°E

5°E
12: NOON

AGONIC LINE

0

1:00 P.M.

5°W

10°W

15°W

20°W

To Convert From:	To Greenwich Mean Time
Eastern Standard Time	Add 5 hours
Eastern Daylight Time	Add 4 hours
Central Standard Time	Add 6 hours
Central Daylight Time	Add 5 hours
Mountain Standard Time	Add 7 hours
Mountain Daylight Time	Add 6 hours
Pacific Standard Time	Add 8 hours
Pacific Daylight Time	Add 7 hours

Figure 2

15. (Refer to Map 3 on Page 101.) What hazards to aircraft may exist in warning areas such as Warning W-50B?

A—Unusual, often invisible, hazards such as aerial gunnery or guided missiles over international waters.

B—High volume of pilot training or unusual type of aerial activity.

C—Heavy military aircraft traffic in the approach and departure area of the North Atlantic Control Area.

16. (Refer to Map 6 on Page 104.) At which airports is fixed-wing Special VFR not authorized?

A—Fort Worth Meacham and Fort Worth Spinks.

B—Dallas-Fort Worth International and Dallas Love Field.

C—Addison and Redbird.

17. (Refer to Map 5, area 3, on Page 103.) The top of the lighted stack approximately 12 nautical miles from the Savannah VORTAC on the 350° radial is

A—305 feet AGL.

B—400 feet AGL.

C—430 feet AGL.

18. (Refer to Map 5 on Page 103.) What is the estimated time en route for a flight from Allendale County Airport (area 1) to Claxton-Evans County Airport (Area 2). The wind is from 090° at 16 knots and the true airspeed is 90 knots. Add 2 minutes for climb-out.

A—33 minutes.

B—37 minutes.

C—41 minutes.

19. (Refer to Map 4 on Page 102.) What course should be selected on the omnibearing selector (OBS) to make a direct flight from Mercer County Regional Airport (area 3) to the Minot VORTAC (area 1) with a TO indication?

A—001°.
B—012°.
C—181°.

20. (Refer to Figure 3.) If the magnetic bearing TO the station is 240°, the magnetic heading is

A—045°.
B—105°.
C—195°.

21. What service should a pilot normally expect from an En Route Flight Advisory Service (EFAS) station?

A—Actual weather information and thunderstorm activity along the route.
B—Preferential routing and radar vectoring to circumnavigate severe weather.
C—Severe weather information, changes to flight plans, and receipt of routine position reports.

22. (Refer to Figure 4.) What is the crosswind component for a landing on Runway 18 if the tower reports the wind as 220° at 30 knots?

A—19 knots.
B—23 knots.
C—30 knots.

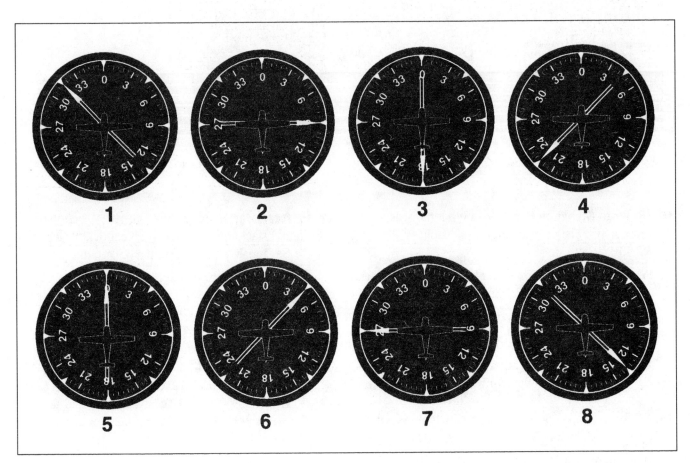

Figure 3

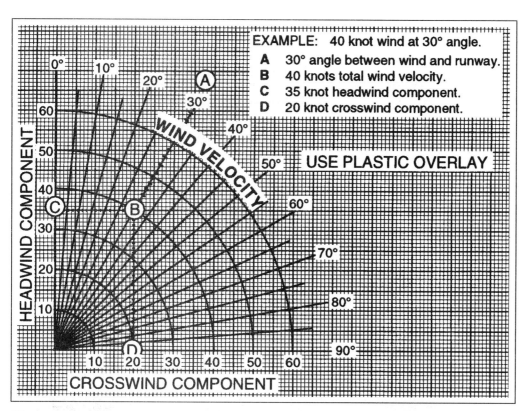

Figure 4

		AT SEA LEVEL & 59 °F		AT 2500 FT & 50 °F		AT 5000 FT & 41 °F		AT 7500 FT & 32 °F	
GROSS WEIGHT LB	APPROACH SPEED, IAS, MPH	GROUND ROLL	TOTAL TO CLEAR 50 FT OBS	GROUND ROLL	TOTAL TO CLEAR 50 FT OBS	GROUND ROLL	TOTAL TO CLEAR 50 FT OBS	GROUND ROLL	TOTAL TO CLEAR 50 FT OBS
1600	60	445	1075	470	1135	495	1195	520	1255

— LANDING DISTANCE —

FLAPS LOWERED TO 40 ° - POWER OFF
HARD SURFACE RUNWAY - ZERO WIND

NOTES: 1. Decrease the distances shown by 10% for each 4 knots of headwind.
2. Increase the distance by 10% for each 60 °F temperature increase above standard.
3. For operation on a dry, grass runway, increase distances (both "ground roll" and "total to clear 50 ft obstacle") by 20% of the "total to clear 50 ft obstacle" figure.

Figure 5

23. (Refer to Figure 5.) Determine the approximate landing ground roll distance.

Pressure altitude .... Sea level
Headwind .... 4 kts
Temperature .... Std

A—356 feet.
B—401 feet.
C—490 feet.

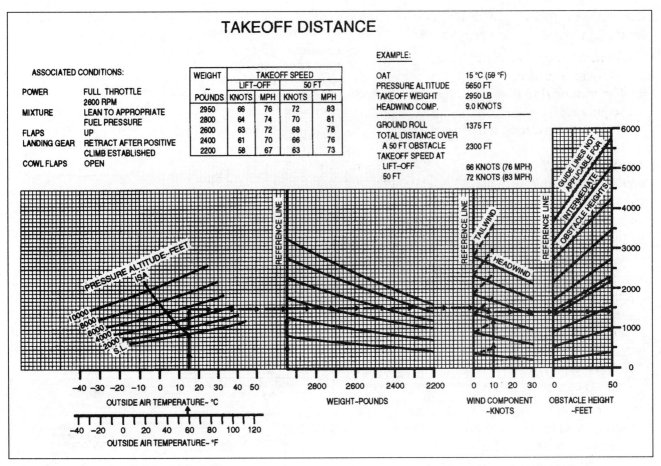

TAKEOFF DISTANCE

EXAMPLE:

OAT	15 °C (59 °F)	
PRESSURE ALTITUDE	5650 FT	
TAKEOFF WEIGHT	2950 LB	
HEADWIND COMP.	9.0 KNOTS	
GROUND ROLL	1375 FT	
TOTAL DISTANCE OVER A 50 FT OBSTACLE	2300 FT	
TAKEOFF SPEED AT		
LIFT-OFF	66 KNOTS (76 MPH)	
50 FT	72 KNOTS (83 MPH)	

ASSOCIATED CONDITIONS:

POWER	FULL THROTTLE 2600 RPM
MIXTURE	LEAN TO APPROPRIATE FUEL PRESSURE
FLAPS	UP
LANDING GEAR	RETRACT AFTER POSITIVE CLIMB ESTABLISHED
COWL FLAPS	OPEN

WEIGHT ~	TAKEOFF SPEED			
	LIFT-OFF		50 FT	
POUNDS	KNOTS	MPH	KNOTS	MPH
2950	66	76	72	83
2800	64	74	70	81
2600	63	72	68	78
2400	61	70	66	76
2200	58	67	63	73

Figure 6

24. (Refer to Figure 6.) Determine the total distance required for takeoff to clear a 50-foot obstacle.

OAT .... Std
Pressure altitude .... 4,000 ft
Takeoff weight .... 2,800 lb
Headwind component .... Calm

A—1,500 feet.
B—1,750 feet.
C—2,000 feet.

25. GIVEN:

	WEIGHT (LB)	ARM (IN)	MOMENT (LB-IN)
Empty weight	1,495.0	101.4	151,593.0
Pilot + passengers	380.0	64.0	—
Fuel (30 gal usable no reserve)	—	96.0	—

The CG is located how far aft of datum?

A—CG 92.44.
B—CG 94.01.
C—CG 119.8.

26. Why is the use of a written checklist recommended for preflight inspection and engine start?

A—To ensure that all necessary items are checked in a logical sequence.

B—For memorizing the procedures in an orderly sequence.

C—To instill confidence in the passengers.

27. When taking off or landing at an airport where heavy aircraft are operating, one should be particularly alert to the hazards of wingtip vortices because this turbulence tends to

A—rise from a crossing runway into the takeoff or landing path.

B—rise into the traffic pattern area surrounding the airport.

C—sink into the flightpath of aircraft operating below the aircraft generating the turbulence.

28. (Refer to Figure 7.) Which runway and traffic pattern should be used as indicated by the wind cone in the segmented circle?

A—Right-hand traffic on Runway 8.

B—Right-hand traffic on Runway 17.

C—Left-hand traffic on Runway 35.

29. (Refer to Figure 8.) VASI lights as shown by illustration C indicate that the airplane is

A—off course to the left.

B—above the glide slope.

C—below the glide slope.

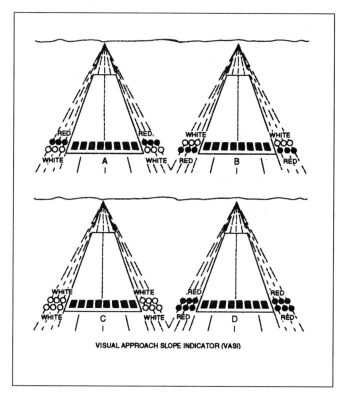

VISUAL APPROACH SLOPE INDICATOR (VASI)

Figure 8

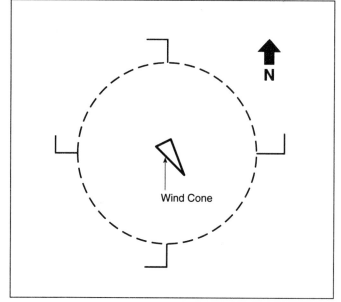

Wind Cone

Figure 7

30. (Refer to Figure 9.) The arrows that appear on the end of the north/south runway indicate that the area

A—may be used only for taxiing.
B—is usable for taxiing, takeoff, and landing.
C—cannot be used for landing, but may be used for taxiing and takeoff.

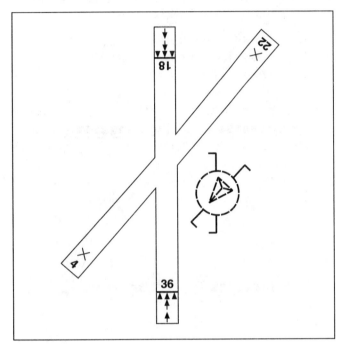

Figure 9

31. Under what condition may an aircraft operate from a satellite airport within Class C airspace?

A—The pilot must file a flight plan prior to departure.
B—The pilot must monitor ATC until clear of the Class C airspace.
C—The pilot must contact ATC as soon as practicable after takeoff.

32. Below FL180, en route weather advisories should be obtained from an FSS on

A—122.0 MHz.
B—122.1 MHz.
C—123.6 MHz.

33. The most effective method of scanning for other aircraft for collision avoidance during nighttime hours is to use

A—regularly spaced concentration on the 3-, 9-, and 12-o'clock positions.
B—a series of short, regularly spaced eye movements to search each 30-degree sector.
C—peripheral vision by scanning small sectors and utilizing offcenter viewing.

34. The letters VHF/DF appearing in the Airport/Facility Directory for a certain airport indicate that

A—this airport is designated as an airport of entry.
B—the Flight Service Station has equipment with which to determine your direction from the station.
C—this airport has a direct-line phone to the Flight Service Station.

35. Rapid or extra deep breathing while using oxygen can cause a condition known as

A—hyperventilation.
B—aerosinusitis.
C—aerotitis.

36. The operator of an aircraft that has been involved in an incident is required to submit a report to the nearest field office of the NTSB

A—within 7 days.
B—within 10 days.
C—when requested.

37. The vertical limit of Class C airspace above the primary airport is normally

A—1,200 feet AGL.
B—3,000 feet AGL.
C—4,000 feet AGL.

38. For private pilot operations, a Second-Class Medical Certificate issued to a 42-year-old pilot on July 15, this year, will expire at midnight on

A—July 15, 2 years later.
B—July 31, 1 year later.
C—July 31, 2 years later.

39. Before a person holding a Private Pilot Certificate may act as pilot-in-command of a high-performance airplane, that person must have

A—passed a flight test in that airplane from an FAA inspector.

B—an endorsement in that person's logbook that he/she is competent to act as pilot-in-command.

C—received flight instruction from an authorized flight instructor who then endorses that person's logbook.

40. What exception, if any, permits a private pilot to act as pilot-in-command of an aircraft carrying passengers who pay for the flight?

A—If the passengers pay all the operating expenses.

B—If a donation is made to a charitable organization for the flight.

C—There is no exception.

41. Flight crewmembers are required to keep their safety belts and shoulder harnesses fastened during

A—takeoffs and landings.

B—all flight conditions.

C—flight in turbulent air.

42. With certain exceptions, when must each occupant of an aircraft wear an approved parachute?

A—When a door is removed from the aircraft to facilitate parachute jumpers.

B—When intentionally pitching the nose of the aircraft up or down 30° or more.

C—When intentionally banking in excess of 30°.

43. What action is required when two aircraft of the same category converge, but not head-on?

A—The faster aircraft shall give way.

B—The aircraft on the left shall give way.

C—Each aircraft shall give way to the right.

44. No person may operate an aircraft in acrobatic flight when the flight visibility is less than

A—3 miles.

B—5 miles.

C—7 miles.

45. If the control tower uses a light signal to direct a pilot to give way to other aircraft and continue circling, the light will be

A—flashing red.

B—steady red.

C—alternating red and green.

46. To determine the expiration date of the last annual aircraft inspection, a person should refer to the

A—Airworthiness Certificate.

B—Registration Certificate.

C—aircraft maintenance records.

47. A 100-hour inspection was due at 3302.5 hours on the tachometer. The 100-hour inspection was actually done at 3309.5 hours. When is the next 100-hour inspection due?

A—3312.5 hours.

B—3402.5 hours.

C—3409.5 hours.

48. Which records or documents shall the owner or operator of an aircraft keep to show compliance with an applicable Airworthiness Directive?

A—Aircraft maintenance records.

B—Airworthiness Certificate and Pilot's Operating Handbook.

C—Airworthiness and Registration Certificates.

49. A temperature inversion would most likely result in which weather condition?

A—Clouds with extensive vertical development above an inversion aloft.

B—Good visibility in the lower levels of the atmosphere and poor visibility above an inversion aloft.

C—An increase in temperature as altitude is increased.

50. What causes variations in altimeter settings between weather reporting points?

A—Unequal heating of the Earth's surface.

B—Variation of terrain elevation.

C—Coriolis force.

51. What would decrease the stability of an air mass?

A—Warming from below.
B—Cooling from below.
C—Decrease in water vapor.

52. What cloud types would indicate convective turbulence?

A—Cirrus clouds.
B—Nimbostratus clouds.
C—Towering cumulus clouds.

53. Which conditions result in the formation of frost?

A—The temperature of the collecting surface is at or below freezing when small droplets of moisture fall on the surface.
B—The temperature of the collecting surface is at or below the dewpoint of the adjacent air and the dewpoint is below freezing.
C—The temperature of the surrounding air is at or below freezing when small drops of moisture fall on the collecting surface.

54. What situation is most conducive to the formation of radiation fog?

A—Warm, moist air over low, flatland areas on clear, calm nights.
B—Moist, tropical air moving over cold, offshore water.
C—The movement of cold air over much warmer water.

55. AIRMETs are issued as a warning of weather conditions particularly hazardous to which aircraft?

A—Small single-engine aircraft.
B—Large multi-engine aircraft.
C—All aircraft.

56. (Refer to Figure 10.) Between 1000Z and 1200Z the visibility at KMEM is forecast to be?

A—1/2 statute mile.
B—3 statute miles.
C—6 statute miles.

57. (Refer to Figure 11.) What hazards are forecast in the Area Forecast for TN, AL, and the coastal waters?

A—Thunderstorms with severe or greater turbulence, severe icing, and low-level wind shear.
B—Moderate rime icing above the freezing level to 10,000 feet.
C—Moderate turbulence from 25,000 to 38,000 feet due to the jetstream.

```
TAF

KMEM   121720Z 121818 20012KT 5SM HZ BKN030 PROB40 2022 1SM TSRA OVC008CB
       FM2200 33015G20KT P6SM BKN015 OVC025 PROB40 2202 3SM SHRA
       FM0200 35012KT OVC008 PROB40 0205 2SM -RASN BECMG 0608 02008KT NSW BKN012
        BECMG 1012 00000KT 3SM BR SKC TEMPO 1214 1/2SM FG
       FM1600 VRB04KT P6SM NSW SKC=

KOKC   051130Z 051212 14008KT 5SM BR BKN030 TEMPO 1316 1 1/2SM BR
       FM1600 16010KT P6SM NSW SKC BECMG 2224 20013G20KT 4SM SHRA OVC020
        PROB40 0006 2SM TSRA OVC008CB BECMG 0608 21015KT P6SM NSW SCT040=
```

Figure 10

```
DFWH FA Ø41Ø4Ø
HAZARDS VALID UNTIL Ø423ØØ
OK TX AR LA TN MS AL AND CSTL WTRS
FLT PRCTNS...TURBC...TN AL AND CSTL WTRS
            ...ICG...TN
            ...IFR...TX
TSTMS IMPLY PSBL SVR OR GTR TURBC SVR ICG AND LLWS
NON MSL HGTS NOTED BY AGL OR CIG
THIS FA ISSUANCE INCORPORATES THE FOLLOWING AIRMETS STILL IN
EFFECT...NONE.

DFWS FA Ø41Ø4Ø
SYNOPSIS VALID UNTIL Ø5Ø5ØØ
AT 11Z RDG OF HI PRES ERN TX NWWD TO CNTRL CO WITH HI CNTR
OVR ERN TX.  BY Ø5Z HI CNTR MOVS TO CNTRL LA.

DFWI FA Ø41Ø4Ø
ICING AND FRZLVL VALID UNTIL Ø423ØØ
TN
FROM SLK TO HAT TO MEM TO ORD TO SLK
OCNL MDT RIME ICGIC ABV FRZLVL TO 1ØØ. CONDS ENDING BY 17Z.
FRZLVL 8Ø CHA SGF LINE SLPG TO 12Ø S OF A IAH MAF LINE.

DFWT FA Ø41Ø4Ø
TURBC VALID UNTIL Ø423ØØ
TN AL AND CSTL WTRS
FROM SLK TO FLO TO 9ØS MOB TO MEI TO BUF TO SLK
OCNL MDT TURBC 25Ø-38Ø DUE TO JTSTR. CONDS MOVG SLOLY EWD
AND CONTG BYD 23Z.

DFWC FA O41Ø4Ø
SGFNT CLOUD AND WX VALID UNTIL Ø423ØØ... OTLK Ø423ØØ-Ø5Ø5ØØ
IFR...TX
FROM SAT TO PSX TO BRO TO MOB TO SAT
VSBY BLO 3F TIL 15Z.
OK AR TX LA MS AL AND CSTL WTRS
8Ø SCT TO CLR EXCP VSBY BLO 3F TIL 15Z OVR PTNS S CNTRL TX.
OTLK...VFR.
TN
CIGS 3Ø-5Ø BKN IØØ VSBYS OCNLY 3-5F BCMG AGL 4Ø-5Ø SCT TO
CLR BY 19Z. OTLK...VFR.
```

Figure 11

58. (Refer to Figure 12.) What is the status of the front that extends from New Mexico to Indiana?

A—Stationary.
B—Occluded.
C—Retreating.

59. (Refer to Figure 13.) If the terrain elevation is 1,295 feet MSL, what is the height above ground level of the base of the ceiling?

A—505 feet AGL.
B—1,295 feet AGL.
C—6,586 feet AGL.

60. (Refer to Figure 14, area D.) What is the direction and speed of movement of the radar return?

A—Southeast at 30 knots.
B—Northeast at 20 knots.
C—West at 30 knots.

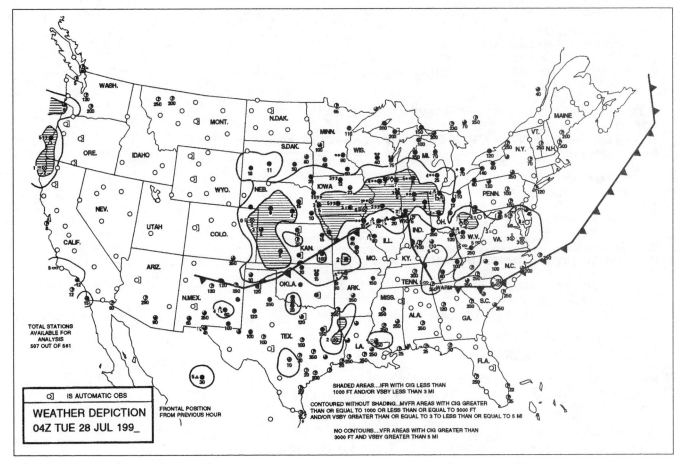

WEATHER DEPICTION
04Z TUE 28 JUL 199_

c⊐ IS AUTOMATIC OBS

FRONTAL POSITION
FROM PREVIOUS HOUR

TOTAL STATIONS
AVAILABLE FOR
ANALYSIS
507 OUT OF 561

SHADED AREAS....IFR WITH CIG LESS THAN
1000 FT AND/OR VSBY LESS THAN 3 MI

CONTOURED WITHOUT SHADING...MVFR AREAS WITH CIG GREATER
THAN OR EQUAL TO 1000 OR LESS THAN OR EQUAL TO 3000 FT
AND/OR VSBY GREATER THAN OR EQUAL TO 3 TO LESS THAN OR EQUAL TO 5 MI

NO CONTOURS....VFR AREAS WITH CIG GREATER THAN
3000 FT AND VSBY GREATER THAN 5 MI

Figure 12

```
UA /OV OKC–TUL /TM 1800 /FL 120 /TP BE90 /SK 018 BKN 055 /
/072 OVC 089 /CLR ABV /TA –9/WV 0921/TB MDT 055–072 /IC LGT–MDT
CLR 072–089.
```

Figure 13

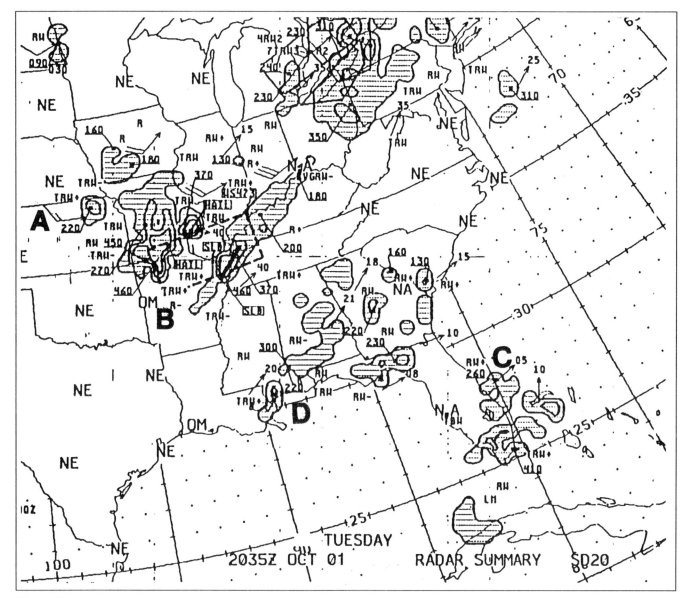

Figure 14

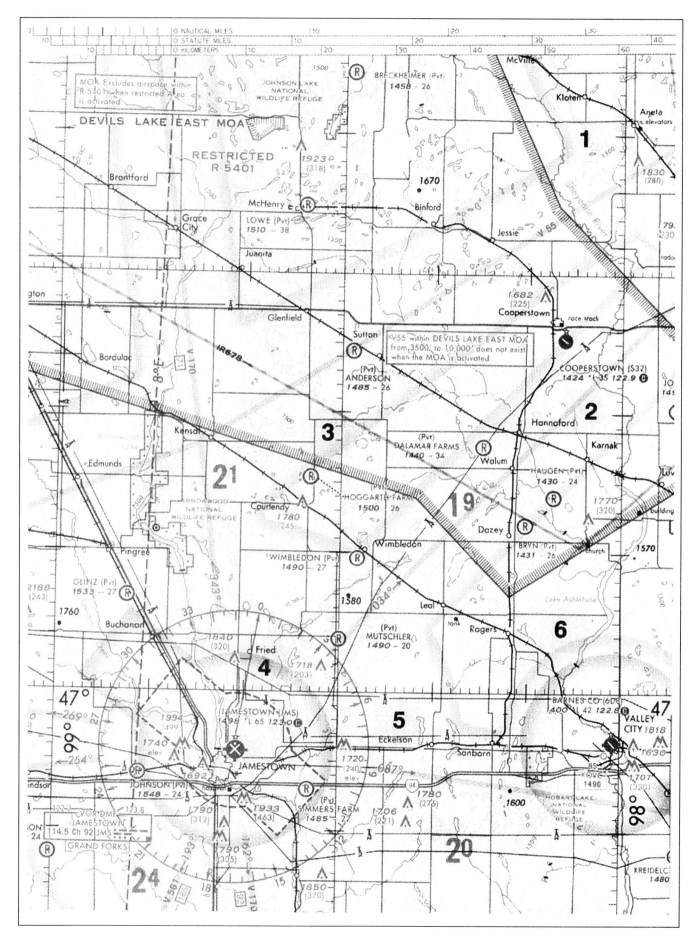

Map 1   99

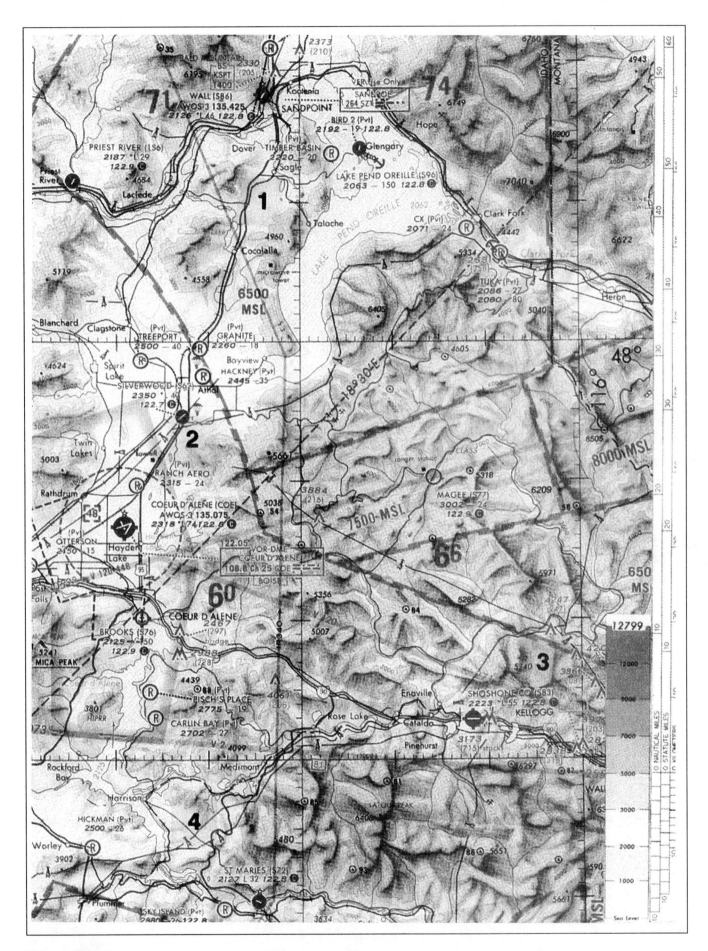

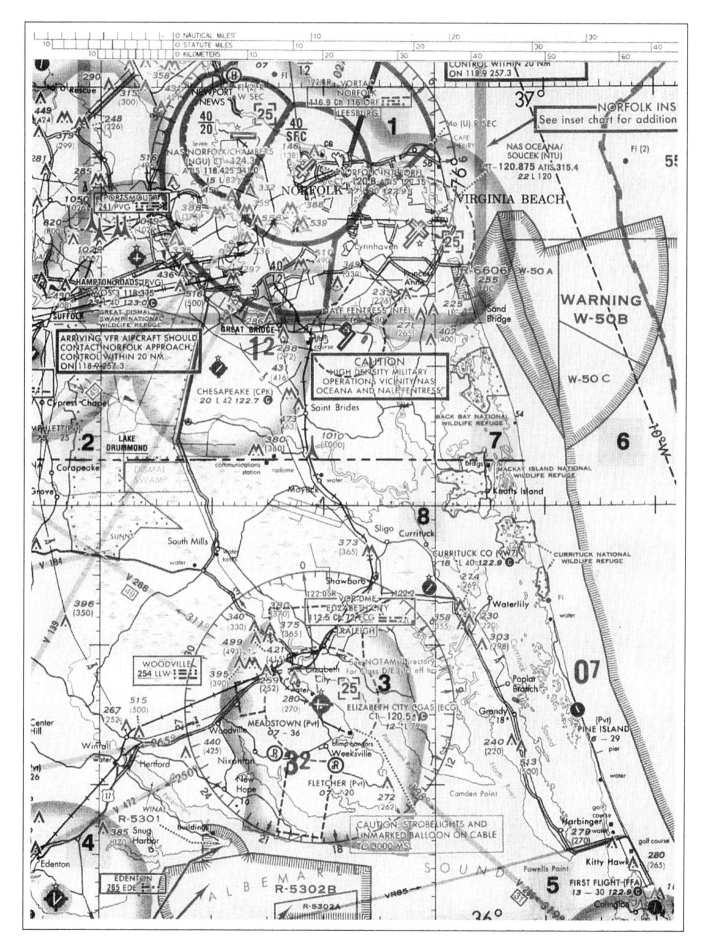

Map 3   101

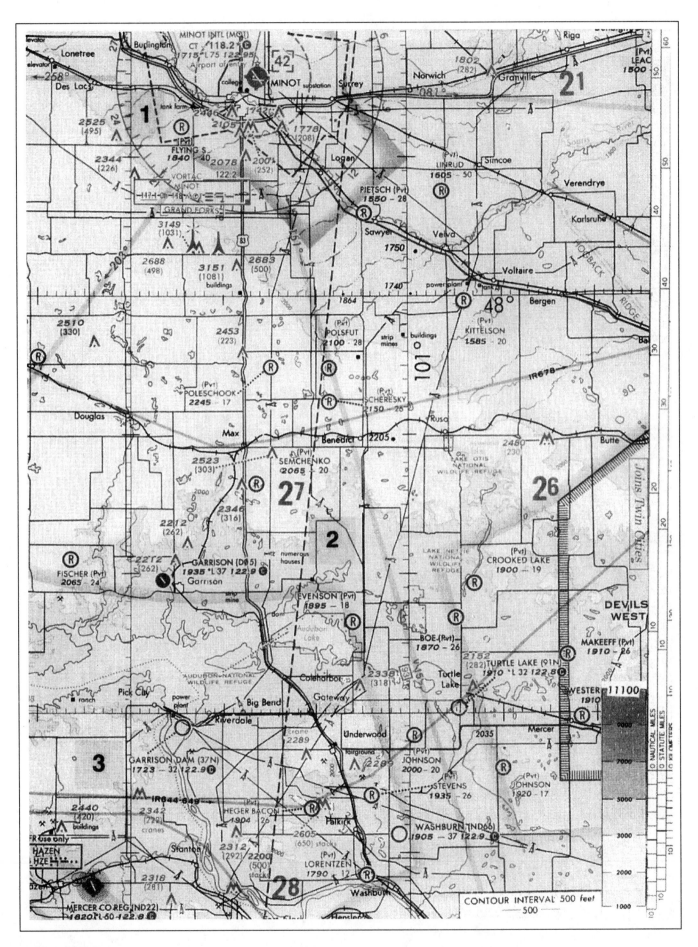

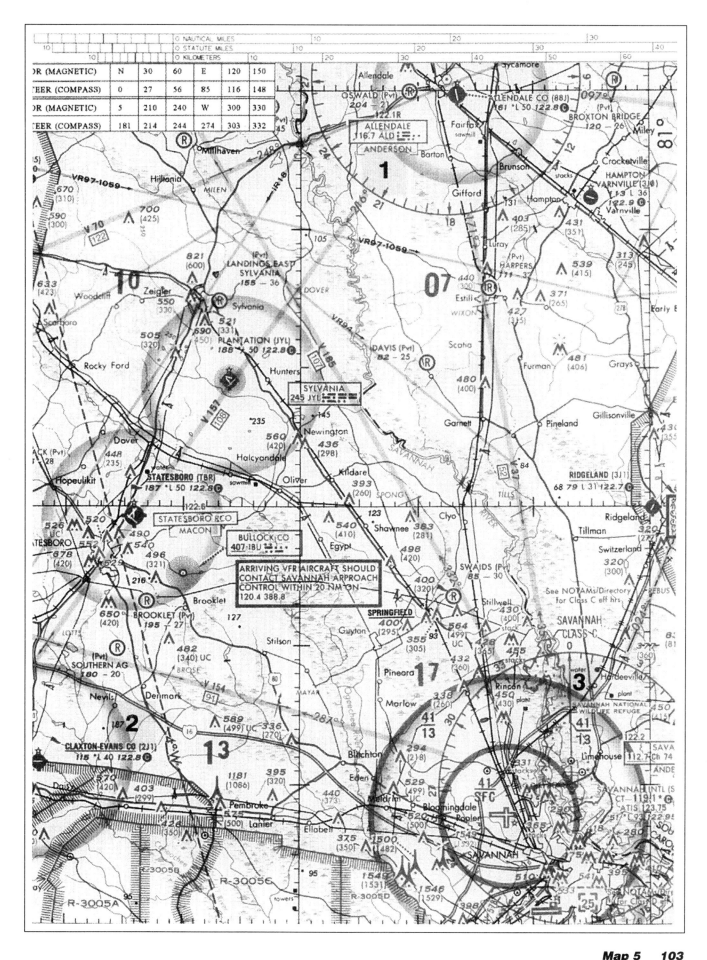

Map 5   103

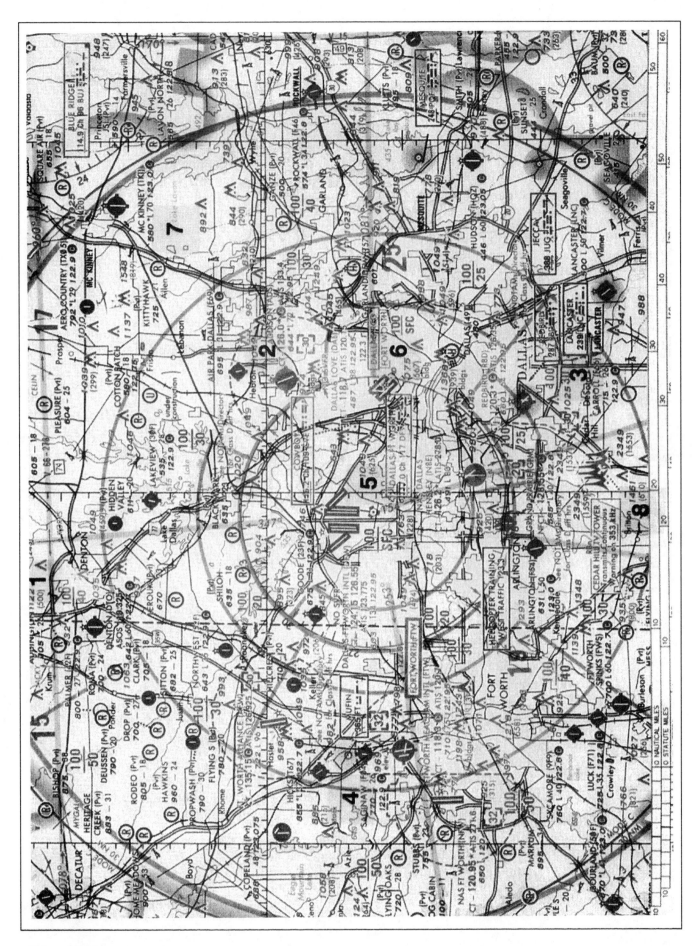

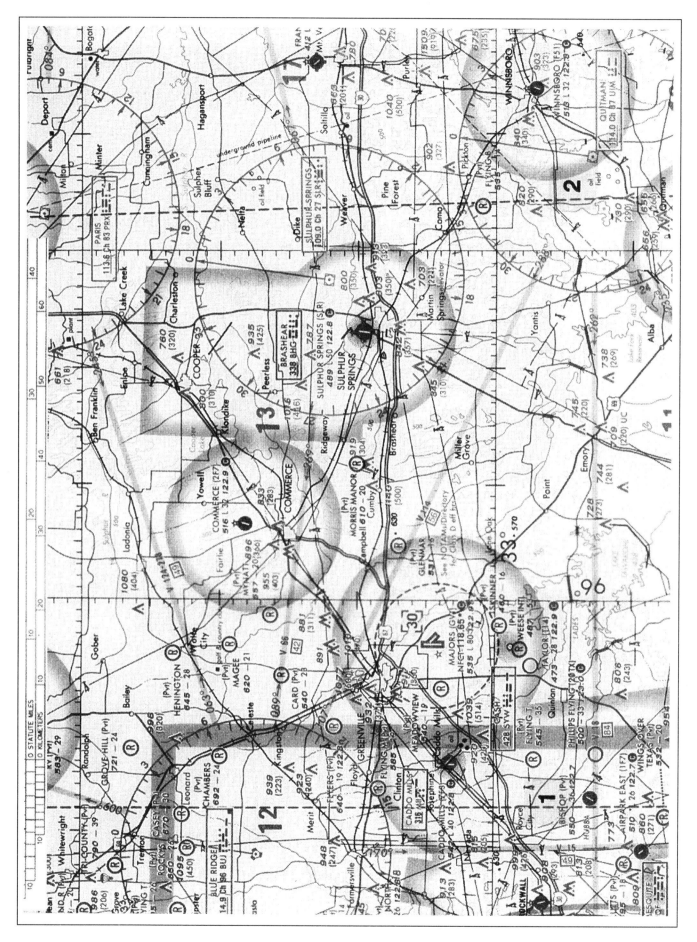

Map 7   105

Appendix

	Page
Answers to Exam Questions	Appendix–3
Enrollment Certificate	Appendix–5
Graduation Certificate	Appendix–5
FAA Form 8710-1	Appendix–6

Answers to Exam Questions

Pre-Solo Exam: Answers

1.	C	9.	A	17.	B	25.	A
2.	C	10.	B	18.	A	26.	A
3.	C	11.	A	19.	C	27.	X
4.	C	12.	A	20.	C	28.	X
5.	A	13.	B	21.	A	29.	X
6.	B	14.	C	22.	B	30.	X
7.	A	15.	B	23.	B		
8.	B	16.	C	24.	B		

Stage Exams: Answers

Stage 1

1.	A	36.	C	14.	A	49.	C
2.	B	37.	C	15.	A	50.	A
3.	B	38.	A	16.	C	51.	A
4.	A	39.	B	17.	C	52.	C
5.	C	40.	B	18.	B	53.	C
6.	A	41.	A	19.	B	54.	B
7.	C	42.	B	20.	C	55.	A
8.	B	43.	A	21.	B	56.	C
9.	A	44.	A	22.	B	57.	C
10.	A	45.	B	23.	A	58.	C
11.	C	46.	B	24.	A	59.	B
12.	C	47.	B	25.	A	60.	C
13.	C	48.	C	26.	C	61.	B
14.	A	49.	C	27.	A	62.	C
15.	A	50.	B	28.	A	63.	C
16.	B	51.	B	29.	B	64.	A
17.	C	52.	B	30.	B	65.	A
18.	C	53.	B	31.	A	66.	A
19.	B	54.	B	32.	B	67.	A
20.	C			33.	A	68.	A
21.	A	**Stage 2**		34.	A	69.	B
22.	C			35.	B	70.	C
23.	B			36.	A	71.	C
24.	C	1.	A	37.	A	72.	A
25.	C	2.	C	38.	B	73.	C
26.	A	3.	A	39.	B	74.	C
27.	C	4.	C	40.	B	75.	B
28.	A	5.	B	41.	A		
29.	C	6.	B	42.	C	**Stage 3**	
30.	B	7.	C	43.	A		
31.	B	8.	C	44.	B		
32.	A	9.	C	45.	C	1.	C
33.	B	10.	C	46.	B	2.	B
34.	A	11.	A	47.	B	3.	C
35.	C	12.	C	48.	A		
		13.	B				

Continued

4. C	16. C	28. C	40. A
5. B	17. C	29. C	41. C
6. C	18. B	30. B	42. B
7. B	19. C	31. B	43. C
8. B	20. B	32. A	44. A
9. C	21. A	33. A	45. A
10. C	22. B	34. A	46. B
11. A	23. C	35. C	47. A
12. C	24. C	36. C	48. B
13. B	25. C	37. C	49. C
14. B	26. A	38. C	50. C
15. A	27. A	39. B	

Final Exam: Answers

1. B	19. A	37. C	55. A
2. B	20. C	38. C	56. B
3. B	21. A	39. C	57. C
4. A	22. A	40. B	58. A
5. A	23. B	41. A	59. A
6. B	24. B	42. B	60. B
7. A	25. B	43. B	
8. B	26. A	44. A	
9. B	27. C	45. B	
10. B	28. C	46. C	
11. A	29. B	47. B	
12. B	30. C	48. A	
13. A	31. C	49. C	
14. C	32. A	50. A	
15. A	33. C	51. A	
16. B	34. B	52. C	
17. B	35. A	53. B	
18. B	36. C	54. A	

Enrollment Certificate

$\mathscr{T}$his is to certify that

_____

Student Name

is enrolled in the Federal Aviation Administration approved
Private Pilot Certification Course, conducted by

_____

School and Certificate Number

_____   _____

Chief Instructor   Date of Enrollment

Graduation Certificate

$\mathscr{T}$his is to certify that

_____

Pilot Name and Number

has satisfactorily completed each required stage of the approved
course of training including the tests for those stages, and has
received _____ hours of cross-country training.

_____ has graduated from the

Federal Aviation Administration approved **Private Pilot
Certification Course** conducted by

_____

School and Certificate Number

_____   _____

Chief Instructor   Date of Graduation

U.S. Department
of Transportation
**Federal Aviation
Administration**

FAA Form 8710-1, Airman Certificate
and/or Rating Application
Supplemental Information and Instructions

Paperwork Reduction Act Statement:

The information collected on this form is necessary to determine applicant eligibility for airman ratings. We estimate it will take 15 minutes to complete this form. The information collected is required to obtain a benefit and becomes part of the Privacy Act system of records DOT/FAA 847, General Air Transportation Records on Individuals. Please note that an agency may not conduct or sponsor, and a person is not required to respond to, a collection of information unless it displays a currently valid OMB control number. The OMB control number associated with this collection is 2120-0021.

Privacy Act

The information on the accompanying form is solicited under authority of Title 14 of the Code of Federal Regulations (14 CFR), Part 61. The purpose of this data is to be used to identify and evaluate your qualifications and eligibility for the issuance of an airman certificate and/or rating. Submission of all requested data is mandatory, except for the Social Security Number (SSN) which is voluntary. Failure to provide all the required information would result in you not being issued a certificate and/or rating. The information would become part of the Privacy Act system of records DOT/FAA 847, General Air Transportation Records on Individuals. The information collected on this form would be subject to the published routine uses of DOT/FAA 847. Those routine uses are: (a) To provide basic airmen certification and qualification information to the public upon request. (b) To disclose information to the national Transportation Safety Board (NTSB) in connection with its investigation responsibilities. (c) To provide information about airmen to Federal, state, and local law enforcement agencies when engaged in the investigation and apprehension of drug violators. (d) To provide information about enforcement actions arising out of violations of the Federal Aviation regulations to government agencies, the aviation industry, and the public upon request. (e) To disclose information to another Federal agency, or to a court or an administrative tribunal, when the Government or one of its agencies is a party to a judicial proceeding before the court or involved in administrative proceedings before the tribunal.

Submission of your Social Security Number is voluntary. Disclosure of your SSN will facilitate maintenance of your records which are maintained in alphabetical order and cross-referenced with your SSN and airman certificate number to provide prompt access. In the event of nondisclosure, a unique number will be assigned to your file.

See Privacy Act Information above. Detach this part before submitting form.

Instructions for completing this form (FAA 8710-1) are on the reverse.

If an electronic form is not printed on a duplex printer, the applicant's name, date of birth, and certificate number (if applicable) must be furnished on the reverse side of the application. This information is required for identification purposes. The telephone number and E-mail address are optional.

Tear off this cover sheet before submitting this form.

AIRMAN CERTIFICATE AND/OR RATING APPLICATION
INSTRUCTIONS FOR COMPLETING FAA FORM 8710-1

I. APPLICATION INFORMATION. *Check appropriate blocks(s).*

Block A. Name. Enter legal name. Use no more than one middle name for record purposes. Do not change the name on subsequent applications unless it is done in accordance with 14 CFR Section 61.25. If you do not have a middle name, enter "NMN". If you have a middle initial only, indicate "Initial only." If you are a Jr., or a II, or III, so indicate. If you have an FAA certificate, the name on the application should be the same as the name on the certificate unless you have had it changed in accordance with 14 CFR Section 61.25.

Block B. Social Security Number. Optional: See supplemental Information Privacy Act. Do not leave blank: Use only **US Social Security Number.** Enter either "SSN" or the words "Do not Use" or "None." SSN's are not shown on certificates.

Block C. Date of Birth. Check for accuracy. Enter eight digits; Use numeric characters, i.e., 07-09-1925 instead of July 9, 1925. Check to see that DOB is the same as it is on the medical certificate.

Block D. Place of Birth. If you were born in the USA, enter the city and state where you were born. If the city is unknown, enter the county and state. If you were born outside the USA, enter the name of the city and country where you were born.

Block E. Permanent Mailing Address. Enter residence number and street, P.O. Box or rural route number in the top part of the block above the line. The City, State, and ZIP code go in the bottom part of the block below the line. Check for accuracy. Make sure the numbers are not transposed. FAA policy requires that you use your permanent mailing address. **Justification must be provided on a separate sheet of paper signed and submitted with the application when a PO Box or rural route number is used in place of your permanent physical address. A map or directions must be provided if a physical address is unavailable.**

Block F. Citizenship. Check USA if applicable. If not, enter the country where you are a citizen.

Block G. Do you read, speak, write and understand the English language? Check yes or no.

Block H. Height. Enter your height in inches. Example: 5'8" would be entered as 68 in. No fractions, use whole inches only.

Block I. Weight. Enter your weight in pounds. No fractions, use whole pounds only.

Block J. Hair. Spell out the color of your hair. If bald, enter "Bald." Color should be listed as black, red, brown, blond, or gray. If you wear a wig or toupee, enter the color of your hair under the wig or toupee.

Block K. Eyes. Spell out the color of your eyes. The color should be listed as blue, brown, black, hazel, green, or gray.

Block L. Sex. Check male or female.

Block M. Do You Now Hold or Have You Ever Held An FAA Pilot Certificate? Check yes or no. (NOTE: A student pilot certificate is a "Pilot Certificate.")

Block N. Grade of Pilot Certificate. Enter the grade of pilot certificate (i.e., Student, Recreational, Private, Commercial, or ATP). Do NOT enter flight instructor certificate information.

Block O. Certificate Number. Enter the number as it appears on your pilot certificate.

Block P. Date Issued. Enter the date your pilot certificate was issued.

Block Q. Do You Now Hold A Medical Certificate? Check yes or no. If yes, complete Blocks R, S, and T.

Block R. Class of Certificate. Enter the class as shown on the medical certificate, i.e., 1st, 2nd, or 3rd class.

Block S. Date Issued. Enter the date your medical certificate was issued.

Block T. Name of Examiner. Enter the name as shown on medical certificate.

Block U. Narcotics, Drugs. Check appropriate block. Only check "Yes" if you have actually been convicted. If you have been charged with a violation which has not been adjudicated, check ."No".

Block V. Date of Final Conviction. If block "U" was checked "Yes" give the date of final conviction.

II. CERTIFICATE OR RATING APPLIED FOR ON BASIS OF:
Block A. Completion of Required Test.
1. AIRCRAFT TO BE USED. (If flight test required) – Enter the make and model of each aircraft used. If simulator or FTD, indicate.
2. TOTAL TIME IN THIS AIRCRAFT (Hrs.) – (a) Enter the total Flight Time in each make and model. (b) Pilot-In-Command Flight Time - In each make and model.

Block B. Military Competence Obtained In. Enter your branch of service, date rated as a military pilot, your rank, or grade and service number. In block 4a or 4b, enter the make and model of each military aircraft used to qualify (as appropriate).

Block C. Graduate of Approved Course.
1. NAME AND LOCATION OF TRAINING AGENCY/CENTER. As shown on the graduation certificate. Be sure the location is entered.
2. AGENCY SCHOOL/CENTER CERTIFICATION NUMBER. As shown on the graduation certificate. Indicate if 142 training center.
3. CURRICULUM FROM WHICH GRADUATED. As shown on the graduation certificate.
4. DATE. Date of graduation from indicated course. Approved course graduate must also complete Block "A" COMPLETION OF REQUIRED TEST.

Block D. Holder of Foreign License Issued By.
1. COUNTRY. Country which issued the license.
2. GRADE OF LICENSE. Grade of license issued, i.e., private, commercial, etc.
3. NUMBER. Number which appears on the license.
4. RATINGS. All ratings that appear on the license.

Block E. Completion of Air Carrier's Approved Training Program.
1. Name of Air Carrier.
2. Date program was completed.
3. Identify the Training Curriculum.

III. RECORD OF PILOT TIME. The minimum pilot experience required by the appropriate regulation must be entered. It is recommended, however, that ALL pilot time be entered. If decimal points are used, be sure they are legible. Night flying must be entered when required. You should fill in the blocks that apply and ignore the blocks that do not. Second In Command "SIC" time used may be entered in the appropriate blocks. Flight Simulator, Flight Training Device and PCATD time may be entered in the boxes provided. Total, Instruction received, and Instrument Time should be entered in the top, middle, or bottom of the boxes provided as appropriate.

IV. HAVE YOU FAILED A TEST FOR THIS CERTIFICATE OR RATING? Check appropriate block.

V. APPLICANT'S CERTIFICATION.
   A. SIGNATURE. The way you normally sign your name.
   B. DATE. The date you sign the application.

Form Approved OMB No: 2120-0021

Airman Certificate and/or Rating Application

DEPARTMENT OF TRANSPORTATION
FEDERAL AVIATION ADMINISTRATION

I Application Information
☐ Student ☐ Recreational ☐ Private ☐ Commercial ☐ Airline Transport ☐ Instrument
☐ Additional Rating ☐ Airplane Single-Engine ☐ Airplane Multiengine ☐ Rotorcraft ☐ Balloon ☐ Airship ☐ Glider ☐ Powered-Lift
☐ Flight Instructor ___ Initial ___ Renewal ___ Reinstatement ☐ Additional Instructor Rating ☐ Ground Instructor
☐ Medical Flight Test ☐ Reexamination ☐ Reissuance of _____ certificate ☐ Other _____

A. Name (Last, First, Middle)	B. SSN (US Only)	C. Date of Birth Month Day Year	D. Place of Birth

E. Address	F. Citizenship ☐ USA ☐ Other ___	Specify	G. Do you read, speak, write, & understand the English language? ☐ Yes ☐ No

City, State, Zip Code	H. Height	I. Weight	J. Hair	K. Eyes	L. Sex ☐ Male ☐ Female

M. Do you now hold, or have you ever held an FAA Pilot Certificate? ☐ Yes ☐ No	N. Grade Pilot Certificate	O. Certificate Number	P. Date Issued

Q. Do you hold a Medical Certificate? ☐ Yes ☐ No	R. Class of Certificate	S. Date Issued	T. Name of Examiner

U. Have you ever been convicted for violation of any Federal or State statutes relating to narcotic drugs, marijuana, or depressant or stimulant drugs or substances? ☐ Yes ☐ No	V. Date of Final Conviction

II. Certificate or Rating Applied For on Basis of:

☐ A. Completion of Required Test	1. Aircraft to be used (if flight test required)	2a. Total time in this aircraft / SIM / FTD hours	2b. Pilot in command hours

☐ B. Military Competence Obtained in	1. Service	2. Date Rated	3. Rank or Grade and Service Number
	4a. Flown 10 hours PIC in last 12 months in the following Military Aircraft.	4b. US Military PIC & Instrument check in last 12 months (List Aircraft)	

☐ C. Graduate of Approved Course	1. Name and Location of Training Agency or Training Center		1a. Certification Number
	2. Curriculum From Which Graduated		3. Date

☐ D. Holder of Foreign License issued By	1. Country	2. Grade of License	3. Number
	4. Ratings		

☐ E. Completion of Air Carrier's Approved Training Program	1. Name of Air Carrier	2. Date	3. Which Curriculum ☐ Initial ☐ Upgrade ☐ Transition

III RECORD OF PILOT TIME (Do not write in the shaded areas.)

	Total	Instruction Received	Solo	Pilot in Command (PIC)	Cross Country Instruction Received	Cross Country Solo	Cross Country PIC	Instrument	Night Instruction Received	Night Take-off/ Landings	Night PIC	Night Take-Off/ Landing PIC	Number of Flights	Number of Aero-Tows	Number of Ground Launches	Number of Powered Launches
Airplanes				PIC / SIC			PIC / SIC				PIC / SIC	PIC / SIC				
Rotorcraft				PIC / SIC			PIC / SIC				PIC / SIC	PIC / SIC				
Powered Lift				PIC / SIC			PIC / SIC				PIC / SIC	PIC / SIC				
Gliders																
Lighter Than Air																
Simulator																
Training Device																
PCATD																

IV. Have you failed a test for this certificate or rating? ☐ Yes ☐ No

V. Applicants's Certification -- I certify that all statements and answers provided by me on this application form are complete and true to the best of my knowledge and I agree that they are to be considered as part of the basis for issuance of any FAA certificate to me. I have also read and understand the Privacy Act statement that accompanies this form.

Signature of Applicant	Date

FAA Form 8710-1 (4-00) Supersedes Previous Edition

NSN: 0052-00-682-5007

Instructor's Recommendation

I have personally instructed the applicant and consider this person ready to take the test.

Date	Instructor's Signature (Print Name & Sign)	Certificate No:	Certificate Expires

Air Agency's Recommendation

The applicant has successfully completed our _____ course, and is recommended for certification or rating without further _____ test.

Date	Agency Name and Number	Officials Signature
		Title

Designated Examiner or Airman Certification Representative Report

☐ Student Pilot Certificate Issued (Copy attached)

☐ I have personally reviewed this applicant's pilot logbook and/or training record, and certify that the individual meets the pertinent requirements of 14 CFR Part 61 for the certificate or rating sought.

☐ I have personally reviewed this applicant's graduation certificate, and found it to be appropriate and in order, and have returned the certificate.

☐ I have personally tested and/or verified this applicant in accordance with pertinent procedures and standards with the result indicated below.

☐ Approved -- Temporary Certificate Issued (Original Attached)

☐ Disapproved -- Disapproval Notice Issued (Original Attached)

Location of Test (Facility, City, State)	Duration of Test		
	Ground	Simulator/FTD	Flight

Certificate or Rating for Which Tested	Type(s) of Aircraft Used	Registration No.(s)

Date	Examiner's Signature (Print Name & Sign)	Certificate No.	Designation No.	Designation Expires

Evaluator's Record (Use For ATP Certificate and/or Type Ratings)

	Inspector	Examiner	Signature and Certificate Number	Date
Oral	☐	☐		
Approved Simulator/Training Device Check	☐	☐		
Aircraft Flight Check	☐	☐		
Advanced Qualification Program	☐	☐		

Aviation Safety Inspector or Technician Report

I have personally tested this applicant in accordance with or have otherwise verified that this applicant complies with pertinent procedures, standards, policies, and or necessary requirements with the result indicated below.

☐ Approved -- Temporary Certificate Issued (Original Attached)   ☐ Disapproved -- Disapproval Notice Issued (Original Attached)

Location of Test (Facility, City, State)	Duration of Test		
	Ground	Simulator/FTD	Flight

Certificate or Rating for Which Tested	Type(s) of Aircraft Used	Registration No.(s)

☐ Student Pilot Certificate Issued

☐ Examiner's Recommendation
  ☐ Accepted ☐ Rejected

☐ Reissue or Exchange of Pilot Certificate

☐ Special Medical test conducted -- report forwarded to Aeromedical Certification Branch, AAM-330

☐ Certificate or Rating Based on
  ☐ Military Competence
  ☐ Foreign License
  ☐ Approved Course Graduate
  ☐ Other Approved FAA Qualification Criteria

☐ Flight Instructor   ☐ Ground Instructor
  ☐ Renewal
  ☐ Reinstatement
Instructor Renewal Based on
  ☐ Activity   ☐ Training Course
  ☐ Test   ☐ Duties and Responsibilities

Training Course (FIRC) Name	Graduation Certificate No.	Date

Date	Inspector's Signature (Print Name & Sign)	Certificate No.	FAA District Office

Attachments:
☐ Student Pilot Certificate (Copy)
☐ Knowledge Test Report
☐ Temporary Airman Certificate
☐ Notice of Disapproval
☐ Superseded Airman Certificate

☐ Airman's Identification (ID)

Form of ID _____

Number _____

Expiration Date _____

Telephone Number _____

ID:
Name: _____

Date of Birth: _____

Certificate Number: _____

E-Mail Address _____

FAA Form 8710-1 (4-00) Supersedes Previous Edition

NSN: 0052-00-682-5007

Notes